CUSTOMER DRIVEN

A Revolutionary System for Putting Golden
Handcuffs on Your Customers—To Find
Ones You Never Knew About—And Keep the
Ones You Already Have

LINDA SILVERMAN GOLDZIMER

WITH

GREGORY L. BECKMANN

**Hutchinson
Business
Books**

Copyright © 1989 Linda Silverman Goldzimer

The right of Linda Silverman Goldzimer to be identified as author of this work has been asserted by her in accordance with the Copyright, Designs and Patents Act 1988

First trade edition published in 1989 in the United States of America by Rawson Associates, Macmillan Publishing Company, New York

First published in Great Britain in 1990 by
Hutchinson Business Books Limited
An imprint of Random Century Limited
20 Vauxhall Bridge Road, London SW1V 2SA

Random Century Australia (Pty) Limited
20 Alfred Street, Milsons Point
Sydney, NSW 2061, Australia

Random Century New Zealand Limited
PO Box 40–086, 32–34 View Road, Glenfield
Auckland 10, New Zealand

Century Hutchinson South Africa (Pty) Limited
PO Box 337, Bergvlei 2012, South Africa

British Library Cataloguing in Publication Data

Goldzimer, Linda Silverman
    Customer driven
    1. Marketing by business firms
    I. Title
    658.8
ISBN 0–09–174442–3
ISBN 0–09–174443–1 (p)

Printed and bound in Great Britain by
Mackays of Chatham PLC, Chatham, Kent

CUSTOMER DRIVEN

To my son, Aaron Marc,
the light of my life.

> for the clarity of your mind
> for the depth of your integrity
> for the beauty of your soul
> i love you

Contents

3

Management with a Mission 36

4

Feedback 67

5

Interviewing and Selecting Stellar Staff   *97*

8

Training and Development

9

The Intelligent Loss of Sales

Acknowledgments

Jerry Silverman Millman is my mother. She is one of those rare individuals who expresses her unbounded love in both words and deeds. She voluntarily moved to California for four months to take over many of my personal responsibilities. This released much of my time and energy and enabled me to complete this book. I am very grateful for her help. I am also proud of myself for being able to accept it.

Julie Howell Turner is the Director of Marketing for The Linda Goldzimer Consulting Group. Julie contributed to this book the way she participates in all her significant endeavors—with unusual talent, exceptional integrity, consistent commitment, and high energy. She is a highly valued colleague and trusted friend.

Gregory L. Beckmann is the collaborating writer on this project. Our relationship began as a professional investment and has now matured into a responsive friendship. His skill as a writer "reads" for itself on these subsequent pages.

Toni Sciarra is my editor. She knew what this book needed before I realized it. Her gentle yet deliberate attention to detail is complemented by her ability to consistently articulate an overall direction. Toni is also fun to work with.

Denise Marcil is my literary agent. She is unfailingly supportive, practical, candid, and to the point—and a very good agent.

My colleagues in the National Speakers Association, as always, shared their expertise and time with me so that I could "OPE"— learn from other peoples' experience. And I did.

Aaron Marc Goldzimer is my son. Children of committed professionals deserve special honor and recognition for their many special qualities, not the least of which is their early maturity and self-discipline. They give us their support and share our pride of accomplishment. Aaron exemplifies all of this and more.

Thank you.

Linda

"I'M FIRST"

The Customer-Driven Market

"Business is a series of great opportunities brilliantly disguised as impossible situations."
—AUTHOR UNKNOWN

I am one of those fortunate people who gets to work at what they enjoy most. In my case, the field is speaking. I love to talk. I'm good at it. I get paid for it. Who could ask for anything more?

I talk to corporate and government leaders about a dynamic new system I have developed to help them improve their organizations in today's quick-changing and highly competitive economy.

It's called "I'M FIRST." Who is the "I"? It is your most precious resource: your customer. "I'M FIRST" is an acronym based on seven crucial principles of customer service:

- Integration
- Mission
- Feedback
- Interviewing
- Reward
- Support
- Training

How did I devise that list?

As a corporate consultant, professional speaker, and staff development trainer, I've worked with thousands of managers to make their companies customer-driven. Organizations in every level of business and government have contacted me to teach them the "I'M FIRST" system, which I will share with you in this book. Why do the best companies use this system? Because they know that everything—from the hiring of employees to the design of your order forms to the color you paint your trucks—either will attract new business, or will alienate your customers, *costing you untold losses in sales*.

From Product-Driven to Customer-Driven: The New Competitive Edge

At the beginning of the Industrial Age, factories set the market's priorities. They would create a product and then go out and sell it. As Henry Ford used to say, "People can buy any color car they want, as long as it's black." The economy was *product-driven*.

By the post–World War II era, the economy had become more sophisticated, and *market-driven* forces began to dominate. Potential buyers were segregated into groups, or markets. Surveys of these markets were conducted to determine what products might sell. Companies then produced products in accordance with the data they had received.

The "I'M FIRST" system is the secret to competing in today's customer-driven market. Its principles apply to *your* business, whether that is a law firm, a textile mill, a hospital, a city planning department, a florist, or your individual entrepreneurship.

Today—and in the future—the orientation is toward what the customer wants and needs. *Being market-driven is not enough anymore,* because global competition for the consumer's dollar is stronger than ever and still growing. How well are you adjusting to this new way of doing business?

If you want to be among tomorrow's leaders, today is the day to become customer-driven. This book will provide a blueprint for doing exactly that. In later chapters, examples, exercises, and interviews with top-level executives of the nation's most successful companies will show you:

- Simple, streamlined ways to gear all of your operational systems—sales, production, delivery, and administration—toward megaprofit by patterning them on what the customer wants and needs
- How to examine your firm from the customer's point of view
- How to identify the hundreds of subconscious decisions your customer is making about your business *every day*— and how to turn those decisions in your favor
- How to create a package of *values* to offer to your customer along with your *product*

It's all on these pages, and it can put you on the leading edge of business.

The Impossible Situations That Could Make You a Winner

Today's rapidly changing marketplace presents unlimited opportunities for the insightful executive or entrepreneur. The right customer service philosophy and procedures will give you a leg up on the competition in dealing with these market pressures:

- *Management of information.* Corporate takeovers and mergers can fly or fail depending on the properly timed release and management of information. Product introductions are carefully planned to get the most publicity in the media. Organizational crises are worsened or minimized in part by how skillfully information about the problem is handled. "Managing the downside risk" in times of crisis is a striking challenge for all executives. What you *say* to customers has become just as important as—if not *more* important than—what you *do*.

Chrysler Corporation chairman Lee Iacocca apologized in full-page newspaper ads around the country when his company was reported to have sold demonstrator cars as new ones. "This was dumb, and it won't happen again" was the message. He confronted the issue head-on, and it quickly dissipated. By being his firm's own worst critic, he had declawed his competitors' criticism and boosted customer goodwill.

Johnson & Johnson worked a public relations miracle after containers of its highly successful Tylenol product were poisoned. The firm recalled every bottle of Tylenol from every store in the country—a very expensive gesture, as there was no reason to believe that every bottle had been tampered with. A few months later, it introduced a "tamper-resistant" container, brilliantly turning a financial disaster into a customer safety feature. Today, even peanut butter jars have tamper-resistant seals.

When things went wrong for Chrysler and for Johnson & Johnson, they actually enhanced their profile by using the crisis as a vehicle for showing concern for their customers. Because the "I'M FIRST" system reveals how to concentrate on the goal that delivers the perfect payoff, customer-related fiascos can become opportunities to show your strength.

• *Growth of entrepreneurship.* The astounding growth of small businesses has made the market more fluid, demanding rapid response to keep pace with political shifts, new technologies, and social and economic changes.

Small businesses are creating jobs at a much faster rate than larger businesses are. "Dun & Bradstreet estimates that as many as two-thirds of the jobs that were created in the U.S. in 1986 are to fill the needs of entrepreneurs," wrote Arthur Zelvin in the *Wall Street Journal* (February 2, 1987). Zelvin, president of Shareholder Reports, continued: "*More than half the work force is employed* [italics mine] by companies with fewer than 100 workers."

These firms are small enough to act quickly when they see a new market emerging. They can give their customers the personal touch that large corporations often lose by insulating themselves with rules and procedures. And they are giving each other plenty of competition as well. Using my system, you'll be getting continual feedback from your customers so you can anticipate market shifts quicker than anyone else, whether your firm is large or small.

• *Deregulation*. The airlines, the trucking industry, banking, and "Ma Bell" are not what they were a few short years ago.

For the phone company, deregulation has meant the first competition ever for long distance service.

In the case of airlines, many airports are overcrowded, while other airports and air routes are being dropped from service. Mergers and takeovers have become so frequent that people joke about taking off on one airline and landing, in the same plane, on another.

Savings and loan institutions now offer checking accounts, credit unions issue Visa cards, and automated teller machines are connected to networks that cover several states. Meanwhile, bank closings are occurring at a frightening pace as weaker institutions are squeezed out by their failure to adapt to the complexities of today's market.

Deregulation has bred instability and barracuda-like competitiveness in these industries, and it may soon come to yours. How will your organization respond?

I will show you how incorporating my principles of customer service will distinguish your firm from the rest, and strengthen your hold on a bigger share of your market.

• *Increasing decentralization*. A study done for the U.S. Labor Department and reported in the *Wall Street Journal* (August 4, 1987) found that the decline in manufacturing as the mainstay of the U.S. economy will alter job locations, hours, and pay. Service jobs, the Hudson Institute study found, "tend to be located *where and when the customer wants them* [italics mine] rather than centralized, as in manufacturing." This will mean fewer people at each workplace, so more and more of your employees will be interacting with customers. Each employee has the potential to make or break the customer relationship because, in the customer's mind, that employee personifies the entire company. "I'M FIRST" will help you take advantage of this extraordinary opportunity to get and keep business.

• *The U.S. trade imbalance and declining dollar.* These factors make American companies less competitive in foreign markets. They also bring foreign companies here to compete with you for *your* customers. As consumers are forced to choose among relatively undifferentiated products, your competitive edge becomes the *relationship* your customer has with your company. "I'M FIRST" is a step-by-step plan to establish and maintain that relationship.

• *The similarity of products.* Because so many modern products have so much in common, the extras you provide will stand out. The basic Toyota-designed subcompact sedan is now made (with different nameplates) in Japan, California, and South Korea. It is the good reputation and caring attitude of the individual dealership that will make the customer choose one over another. I will demonstrate how to build that reputation and reinforce that attitude throughout your organization.

What are *your* three top competitive pressures? What conditions, people, or businesses are squeezing your bottom line? Write them down now. By the end of this book, you will know how to neutralize these pressures.

The Customer Relationship:
Your Operational Imperative

Given these conditions in today's business world, how do you keep—and enlarge—your competitive edge? By realizing that customers will base more of their choices not on the product, but on *the package of values that comes with the product*.

Many firms already recognize this potent new approach to business. Some are stressing the personal angle in their advertisements. "We're more interested in a long-term business relationship than a one-time deal," a Sanwa Bank California ad declares next to a photo of a caketop bride and bridegroom. "We've got the people and expertise to make a relationship work. So you don't have to marry us just for our money."

"People Make the Difference," reads the June 1987 newspaper ad for Bullock's, a department store in southern California. "We think our people are very special. . . . *We chose them for their eagerness to be of service*" (emphasis mine).

Advertising such as this is a good start. It can bring customers through the door or motivate them to call you. However, what happens next is all-important. The secret is to take the advertising slogan and make it part of *everything* your firm does. "I'M FIRST" shows you how to make customer satisfaction your operational imperative.

You may be thinking, "Many times I cannot give my customers exactly what they want. They may want an exception to the building code that will make the structure unsafe. Sometimes, if I expedite delivery for one customer, it will delay other customers' deliveries, leaving them angry. At times, I do not have the money or the capacity to do what the customer wants. How can I make all my customers happy?"

Clearly, we cannot keep 100 percent of our customers happy 100 percent of the time. In fact, some customers do not even *want* to be satisfied. ("I get emotional gratification from being an irritant and receiving your attention," a customer once told me!)

Most customers know that they cannot always receive exactly what they want. But they still expect responsive, caring, knowledgeable, flexible attitudes and behavior. They want a reply that seeks alternate pathways to reach the goal of solving their problems—solutions that both you and the customer can live with. If they experience this, they are "satisfied," even when you cannot give them what they initially wanted.

Your goal, then, is to make your customer *feel good about doing business with you*. The "I'M FIRST" system gives you a step-by-step process for creating an organization that continually achieves this.

Who Is Your Customer?

I define a customer as someone who, driven by self-interest, has the choice of coming to you for your product or service or going somewhere else. In government, the unhappy customer cannot go somewhere else—but he can vent his frustration through ballot initiatives, by rejecting bond issues, and by griping to the City Council, all of which can make your managerial life just as miserable as lost sales can for a businessman's.

"I'M FIRST" applies to firms that produce a tangible product, such as environmental monitoring equipment, automotive parts, or computers. And it applies to those that produce a "service product," such as attorneys, agents, stockbrokers, government officials, and financial consultants. The system will succeed for every manager or entrepreneur who works with passengers, patrons, buyers, riders, clients, guests, students, patients, audiences, or supervisors and voters.

I have been advocating good customer service in speaking engagements and published articles for years. I talk about it on TV and radio.

My consulting, speaking, and training services have been retained by a wide variety of public and private organizations: from an automobile dealership to a big-eight accounting firm, from a huge county fair to a small northern California town, from a top-of-the-line hotel complex to a medium-sized police department, from a very large hard equipment manufacturer to conventions and conferences of all kinds.

Bottom-line benefits of the "I'M FIRST" system include:

- Bigger profits/greater recognition
- More customer/constituent support
- Less employee turnover
- Higher productivity
- Adaptability to changing market/community conditions
- Better internal communications and cooperation (and therefore less time and money wasted in misunderstandings and duplication of effort)

What Is "I'M FIRST"?

Local governments and many companies often try to improve "customer service" by treating it as a separate department like engineering or manufacturing, training a tiny segment of the staff to become the complaint department. This is a Band-Aid approach. And it will not work. What is needed (and what I can promise) is a total transformation.

"I'M FIRST" involves a total INTEGRATION of service to the customer throughout every floor, every department, every facet of your organization. As you will discover in chapter 2, everybody must be involved in this, not just the "customer-contact people."

For that to happen, top management must set the example by being the number one customer service advocates. Chapter 3 will explain how to do this by instilling managers with the MISSION of forging a companywide commitment to customer relationships.

Then I will show you how to set up a FEEDBACK system that will keep you up to date on what is evolving in the marketplace. Your customers will tell you how to be successful, if you will only listen to them. More importantly, the feedback chapter reveals how to receive the information in a meaningful form—so you can easily act on it.

INTERVIEWING and selecting the right people are essential to good customer service. Hiring is expensive (and firing someone is even more costly). Chapter 5 shows you how to build a quality team with the required attitude.

To sustain the performance you need, I recommend a system of REWARDS for your employees. The reward may be monetary, or it may be the freedom to go home half an hour early every day for a week. What matters is that you reward the top performers in a way that exerts upward pressure on their performance with the customer, as well as boosting morale.

My next point is vital to the "I'M FIRST" system, but it is often treated very casually by management: SUPPORT for your employees. It means giving employees the freedom *and responsibility* to decide the appropriate response to a customer's complaint. It includes providing the proper equipment and sufficient staffing. It means creating a company where your employees actually can do what you want them to do.

TRAINING is the final component of my system. I'm not talking about technical training here. You are the best judge of the technical skills that your employees need to run the earth mover, close the sale, negotiate the loan, or fill out the forms. I am concerned with the people dimension of the job. You are responsible for developing your staff's skills in this area, too. Without these skills, the bonding necessary for continued customer satisfaction simply does not take place. All the technical training in the world will be for naught if disgruntled customers are dropping you in droves.

What Will It Cost?

I want to stress that, as you turn your company into a customer-driven one, *the cost should be minimal*. My system involves a redeployment of monies *already being spent*.

Everything in "I'M FIRST" that might have a price tag—feedback, interviewing, reward, support, and training—is already being done, in one form or another, as part of your day-to-day business. To make your agency customer-driven, you need only refocus and reinvest your resources, not necessarily make substantial new investments. Like your personal investments in the stock market, in bonds, or in certificates of deposit, you just move the money around to get higher returns.

Of course, while evaluating and redesigning your firm, you may very well conclude that you need a new phone system, a new computer, or new software to measure your performance. Spending that money may be the best way to solve a problem and give your staff the support they need to get the job done. It becomes a choice of paying a known amount now as an investment in yourself and your company, or paying untold amounts later in the form of lost business, missed opportunities, and decreased constituent support.

What's in It for You?

Gaining and keeping customer allegiance is just good business. For instance, a 1974 survey of 100 top U.S. companies, conducted by Drake, Sheehan/Stewart, Dougall, Inc., a management consulting firm, found that it is "six times more expensive to acquire a new customer than to keep present ones." *Six times!* If you can afford to throw away all but every sixth dollar, send them to me, please!

"A satisfied, happy client is the best reference you'll ever have," declares Ira Gottfried, an executive partner with the Big Eight accounting and management consulting firm of Coopers & Lybrand. A prospective client is more likely to do business with you if he knows you have a good relationship with his golfing partner.

Companies depend heavily on repeat sales. "Firms selling services depend on existing customers for 85 to 95 percent of their business," educators and writers E. Patricia Birsner and Ronald Balsley state in *Practical Guide to Customer Service*

*Management and Operations.** "Firms selling durable products require in excess of 65 percent resale to be profitable." Your organization would soon be history if two-thirds of your customers gave up on you because your competitors gave them better service.

Having a good customer relationship beats the most expensive market research because your customers will tell you what they want. Lawrence Sills, president of Standard Motor Products of Long Island City, New York, told me this story. His company, which has 3,000 employees and $250 million in annual revenue, controls 30 percent of the market he supplies in automotive replacement parts.

Standard received a call for a part that it normally sells about 100 of each month. The customer needed *2,000* of them.

"We have only three hundred, and you can't have all of these" was the Standard employee's reply. The customer contacted a competitor of Standard and got the parts he needed. But because of his long-standing relationship with Standard Motor Products, he called Sills and told him, in so many words, "Your people screwed up."

From that one call about a lost sale, Sills learned that he had an employee who didn't understand "I'M FIRST," and that he needed more flexibility in inventory control so the firm could respond to its customers' needs. If you will listen, your customers will do your market research for you. This feedback is part of the "F" in my "I'M FIRST" system.

Service is also very important in the customer's eyes. A study published by the National Council of Physical Distribution Management (Chicago, 1976) found that customers would reduce purchases by 22.4 percent if customer service standards fell by just 5 percent. Imagine, then, what could happen if you *increased* service by just 5 percent!

*E. Patricia Birsner and Ronald Balsley, *Practical Guide to Customer Service Management and Operations* (New York: AMACOM, a division of the American Management Association, 1982). Used by permission.

> Good customer service shows up on your bottom line.

To help you maintain and increase your market share, this book will:

- Outline cost-effective methods to improve your relationships with existing customers as well as gain new ones
- Give you a people-to-people program that is accessible, practical, and ready for you—the busy manager or entrepreneur—to use
- Provide dozens of examples, ideas, and suggestions that leading businesses have used successfully to improve service, with inside information from high-level decision-makers explaining exactly how they did so

"I'M FIRST" is a workable system that applies to the real world of project deadlines, incessant interruptions, creative challenges, and "impossible" situations. It is *the* way to make your company stand out in the crowded international marketplace of the 1990s and beyond.

2

Integration

"Quite Simply the Best"™
———BOCA RATON HOTEL AND CLUB

W hen I first met Ted Kleisner, he was president of Florida's renowned Boca Raton Hotel and Club.* His was a small office, tucked away in the 1,100-room resort complex. In beige and brown, it had almost no definable decor. A table with four chairs. A couple of armchairs. A desk. It seemed to have been carved out of leftover space, almost as an afterthought: "Oh, yes, the president will need an office."

On one wall were pictures of bearded men from the last century, standing on the porches of wood-frame buildings. This is Ted Kleisner's heritage. These are all hotel people, three generations of them.

A tall, sandy-haired man, Kleisner struck me as having an impressive ability to focus on the matter at hand, setting everything else aside. As I settled into an armchair in his Boca Raton office, I was, for the moment, the center of his attention. He seemed composed, confident and self-contained.

"Quite Simply the Best"™ is "the level of expectation that

---

*Kleisner currently is vice-president and managing director of The Greenbrier in White Sulphur Springs, West Virginia, a 200-year-old resort with a five-diamond AAA rating and a five-star Mobil rating.

the guest has coming through the door," Kleisner told me. It is a promise of what will be delivered by each and every department of the Boca Raton Hotel and Club.

This trademark is not just the hotel's advertising slogan. It is the *integrating force* that unifies 2,000 employees spread over 250 acres at four different sites. "Quite Simply the Best"™ is on the hotel's stationery. It is emblazoned on walls and menus— even on the hotel postcards sold in the lobby. It is considered when every decision is made, when every reservation is made, when every bed is made.

In the true spirit of "I'M FIRST"'s concept of total integration, nothing that influences the guest's perception of the hotel is left to chance. Kleisner even translated "Quite Simply the Best"™ into a written standard "for every component of the resort experience."

He elaborated, "If we are going to have towels on the beach that cover the cabana pads, then a standard is written that the towel is a certain size: It's a bath sheet, seventy-two inches by four feet. It has a certain cotton requirement, so many threads per square inch. Then there is an employee training standard on how a person is to be greeted and how they are to be offered the towel."

Kleisner understands that the guest is evaluating every nuance of the staff's behavior to see if it measures up to "Quite Simply the Best."™ At the Beach Club, the desk receptionist who greets you when you check in also escorts you to your room. She is trained in the geography of the entire resort, in what to say while walking to your room, and in how to exit gracefully.

Because Kleisner has *integrated* "Quite Simply the Best"™ into every task the hotel staff performs, it becomes a self-fulfilling prophecy. Like a heat-seeking missile, which constantly adjusts its flight path toward its target, each employee attunes his actions to the hotel's goal. Each understands that good service is expected, that exceptional service will be rewarded and that bad service will harm the company's reputation. Thus, there is constant upward pressure on improving service.

> You customer service philosophy will create a vital *cohesiveness* within your organization.

"This must cost a lot of money," you may be thinking. "That's great for a swanky hotel in Florida, but how does this service concept apply to me?"

Providing an upscale environment is not the issue. You don't have to have the silk carpets, prize-winning landscaping, and elegant china that Kleisner's customers expect. At a machine shop, where customers arrive in their work clothes, a more informal, relaxed atmosphere is more appropriate and will encourage more business. What matters is how you deliver *your* product or service to *your* customer.

The "I'M FIRST" system applies to businesses servicing high-end, mid-range, and low-end markets. It won't work for companies trying to sell the same way to all three because *those companies won't work*.

Figure out what makes your customers feel comfortable and adjust your set-up accordingly. Go into any bank just about anywhere, for example, and you'll see that the vault door is open during business hours. While they wait to make a transaction, customers can measure the thickness of the enormous vault door. Glass reveals the complex mechanism of the lock. Its dials and gears are polished and gleaming. The door must weigh four tons.

"The impression is one of security and impenetrability," says Joe Turner, senior vice-president and human resources director of Home Federal Savings and Loan, the nation's eleventh-largest banking institution, with $12 billion in assets.

Banks don't really need such massive vault doors. With today's alloys, they could easily use thinner, lighter doors and have just as much protection.

"But the customer expects it," continued Turner. "She wants to see that huge door because it makes her feel that her money is secure when it goes in that safe. We keep the huge vault door to make our customers feel good. The door is a symbol of the bank's *relationship* with its customers."

Recognize the lasting symbolic value of the image *your customer perceives* during every contact with your organization. Then take control of that image—don't leave it to chance.

Manage for Total Impact: What You Can Do

Your customer is making *thousands* of subconscious decisions about you and your product every time you, someone, or something representing your company makes contact with her. You are constantly making verbal and nonverbal impressions that can create or destroy this synergism.

Take a moment now to evaluate the impressions a customer of yours would receive at each point of contact with your firm. Your evaluation should encompass *everything* that makes an imprint in the customer's mind, including:

- Product packaging. Is it easy to open or merely cheap for you to produce?
- Advertising. Is it consistent and coordinated, or intermittent and poorly focused?
- The design of your stationery. Splashy or simple? Establishment or avant-garde?
- The furniture in your offices. Ramshackle leftovers or colorful coordinates? Functional or gaudy?
- The way you exhibit your product. Is it easy for you or informative and pleasing to the customer?
- Your field personnel's style of dress or uniforms. Is the image right?

- Your business forms. Are they too long? Too short? Do they match your computer or your customers?
- The way your employees (and you!) answer (or don't answer!) the telephone. *This cannot be overemphasized!* The ringing telephone heralds the start of the customer relationship. Do your company's telephone manners reflect this awareness?

If these image-forming elements conflict with each other, you are not encouraging synergism. Shoddy work in one area is canceling out good work in another.

Here's what I mean by letting your customer's values influence your total service package: The truck that delivers Budweiser beer to the Camp Pendleton Marine Corps base in California is painted camouflage green. "When we're on-base, we get the thumbs-up sign all the time," a company spokesman said. That paint job shows that Budweiser is thinking about its U.S. Marine customers—tailoring even its delivery truck to the Marines' environment.

Write down a note on the "imprint" customers receive from your business as you answer these questions:

- Are there empty soda cans and trash in the front seat of your drivers' trucks? Are the trucks themselves clean? (I've never seen a dirty United Parcel Service truck.)
- How tidy is the receptionist's desk? Is she making personal calls, eating lunch, or reading a romance novel?
- Does your office set-up help the customer find what he needs? Is your staff correctly positioned? Are they standing or seated for maximum effectiveness?
- What message do your signs convey? Do they emphasize what a visitor can do, or what he cannot do? Could an eight-year-old find any department in your complex? (Don't laugh; the signs should be *that* clear.)
- Are the lighting and music suited to the mood you are trying to create?
- Where is the garbage?

Even the design of the physical plant should be geared toward helping the customer. When Dr. Allen D. ("call me 'Skip'") Johnson talks about the Heart, Lung, and Vascular Disease Center that he directs at the world-famous Scripps Clinic & Research Foundation in La Jolla, California, his eyes light up as he describes its layout.

All the physicians—representing cardiology, cardiac surgery, vascular surgery, thoracic surgery, and chest and critical care medicine—have their offices around the periphery of the second floor of the new center. Interspersed among these offices are meeting rooms equipped with the latest viewing and conference equipment. These rooms are used for the formal and informal communications that are the foundation of the center's philosophy of multidisciplinary patient care.

The operating and treatment rooms are on the first level of the building, while the Intensive Care Unit is on the third. A special elevator bypasses the second floor, connecting the operating rooms directly with the Intensive Care Unit.

In the more common "design" of medical facilities, the physicians and other medical and technical experts are scattered over one or more buildings—or even throughout the neighborhood. In the new Scripps facility, the design is consciously planned to benefit the customer/patient by providing an environment where state-of-the-art health care can take place.

See your organization as a total package, or as a series of *reinforcing systems*, designed to serve customers.

I am assuming that the service or product your company provides is of a consistently high quality. Quality is essential to keeping customer allegiance. However, in today's customer-driven marketplace, simply providing high-quality products is not enough.

The newly formed partnership of Honeywell Bull states in its "first" ad that "Customers Are More Important Than Computers."

"We've organized ourselves to work side-by-side with our customers," the ad states. "Not just until the computers are delivered, but continuously until your *problems* are solved." The people at Honeywell Bull know that the *relationship* between the company and its customers is part of what its customers are buying.

Write down the integrating factor that governs your organization today. Ask yourself, "What philosophy is behind what we say, how we look, and what we do?" It's your responsibility to create and manage the total impact that your business has on your client.

Kill the Complaint Department: Complaints Are Everyone's Job

Another aspect of integration is *distributing responsibility for the customer relationship throughout the organization*. Traditionally, customer relations has been compartmentalized into the "complaint department" or the "exchange window." It has been seen more as a necessary evil—"Well, somebody has to handle the complaints"—than as an opportunity to develop new business. In keeping with that philosophy, the complaint department usually has been staffed with high-turnover personnel who are poorly trained, poorly managed, and poorly paid.

When companies handle the focal point of customer contact in that way, thousands of dollars in sales are lost. In effect, these firms are pouring their dollars into advertising to get *new* customers (which, research shows, is *six* times more expensive) while their existing customers are going elsewhere.

I tell my clients, "Kill the complaint department!"

Customer service will never make money for you if it is compartmentalized. Each employee must be involved in serving the customer. She must be ready—and empowered by you through training and support (which I will detail in later chapters)—to respond to customers' complaints and needs.

She cannot tell a customer calling with a problem, "Sorry, I can't help you. You'll have to call the complaint department between one and four P.M. on Monday." People taking orders over the phone, typists sending out letters, clerks handling accounts receivable—*even the people who never talk to a customer*—are all needed to improve your company's customer relationships.

Customer-driven organizations know that service is not an "end-of-the-line" activity in which customer service specialists get involved with the product only after it has been sold. All down the line, everyone in your agency needs to be involved, making customer service a profit generator, not a cost of doing business.

Customer service is not an isolated activity.

A Nordstrom department store has twice the merchandise, twice the salespeople, and twice the number of cash registers of other stores—thus, more fixed overhead—but spends half as much on advertising. In California alone, Nordstrom pays an hourly wage as much as 20 percent higher than its competitors'. On top of that comes an average commission of 6.75 percent. In its forty-five stores in California, Washington, Oregon, Alaska, and Montana, Nordstrom's sales per square foot (the basic performance yardstick in the industry) are *double* the average. How do they do it? Go into a Nordstrom store, and you'll see signs reading, "The only real difference between stores is the way they treat their customers."

Picking your way through the crowd on the main floor is a tantalizing and stimulating experience. The effect of glass chandeliers, marble surfaces, and music from the grand piano beside the escalators is almost lost amid the hum and bustle of shoppers and busy sales personnel. I am at the Nordstrom at South Coast Plaza in Costa Mesa, California. It is Saturday, and the store is full of shoppers.

I'm examining a pink leather belt on a mannequin. I feel a presence behind me and hear, "May I take the belt down for you to see?" I turn to find an attractive brunette, well dressed and with perfect makeup.

This woman, who I assumed was a sales clerk, then undresses the entire mannequin just so I can look at the belt. She was, in fact, the department manager, working the floor as they all do. Service at Nordstrom is not limited to the traditional customer contact personnel. No matter what the person's job or status in the company, service to the customer is that person's highest priority. That's integration at work.

Another store, another story: I was browsing on the main floor of a southern California Nordstrom store. The store manager, Rick, noticed the puzzled look on my face. "How can I help you?" he said. "I am looking for the children's clothes," I responded. Rick accompanied me up the escalator to the third floor, all the while engaging in animated conversation. On the third floor, he gracefully transferred me to a sales associate in children's clothes, introducing both of us by name.

At Nordstrom, the phrase "How can I help you?" is part of everyone's job description. Employees at every level of the organization do not just point to a possible solution to your problem, but *personally assume the responsibility* of leading the way, as Rick did. You don't get referred, jostled, and handed off to an endless line of new clerks. Every person understands that responsibility to the customer is part of his job description.

Everyone in your company must have the responsibility to help the customer.

The "Feel-Good Factor" in Customers' Decisions

Have you ever tried to do business with a company only to run into a particularly difficult staff person? Someone who griped, "You have to be more specific," using an exasperated tone that made you feel that you were interrupting her work? You may have gotten what you were looking for, but only after an unnecessary hassle. Afterward, you probably did what other people do: Based on one negative conversation with one difficult person, you were ready to write off everyone who works there.

Customers generalize from one experience to the entire company.

That is why you must be sure that your employees show the customer that he's the reason everyone came to work in the morning. "You have the wrong department," "He's on a break," "They're in a meeting," or "That's not my job" indicate that someone or something else is more important.

Your customer relations are only as strong as your weakest employee.

The customer called you, wanting some answers. Whoever he reached must be ready, willing, and able to work on that customer relationship. That's integration.

Each transaction should be a transference of good feelings from employee to customer. A 1984 political cartoon by Scrawls in the *Atlanta Constitution* illustrates the power of this concept: A man is lying in a hospital bed. On the left stands a very dour Dr. Walter Mondale. On the right (yes, the Right) is a man dressed in a cheerleader outfit, jumping up and down and holding a megaphone. The "R" on his sweater and the pompadour wave identify him as Ronald Reagan. The dying patient says to Mondale, "Oh, you're probably a better doctor, but he makes me feel good."

If voters can base the election of their president in part on the feelings he generates, those same people will do business with the companies that make them feel good. By developing a consistent, positive way to deal with customers, you can count on the "feel-good factor" to work in your favor when your customers make a buying decision.

> **Customers want to do business with people who make them feel good about themselves and their decisions.**

Get a Broad Perspective: What Are You Really Selling?

Jurg R. Reinshagen is managing director of the Palace Hotel in Lucerne, Switzerland, a five-star beauty of a place in one of the most picturesque cities in the world. He is elegant in manner, stride, and speech, with a seasoned maturity enlivened by a spark of youth.

I had written to Reinshagen, noting that I would like to interview him about service to the customer.

When I arrived to register at the hotel, Mr. Reinshagen was working the front desk, and I was immediately referred to him. He had marked "VIP" on my reservation card, and he addressed me by name.

His style is sincere, with just enough charm. He asked how I was finding Lucerne, and I remarked that I could use some sunshine (it had been a rainy week). His graceful reply was that "it has been ordered, but sometimes the delivery is a little slow." What a way to flatter the customer. The Palace Hotel had ordered sunshine for me!

Compared to modern American chain hotels, the Palace is

small. It has 163 rooms and employs 150 people in its peak season. Yet its ambiance does make the hotel seem like a palace. The furniture is plush, the wallpaper is silk, the fixtures are elegant. The guest immediately senses that this is more than a tasteful shelter from the Swiss chill.

Speaking to me in a comfortable public salon rather than in his office, Reinshagen told me that his mission as a manager is to maintain harmony among the staff: "Each employee should, of course, be extraordinarily helpful to the guests, but *the atmosphere between staff and staff is more important* because that is what generally creates the environment that reflects on the guests."

In most firms, harmony among the staff, if considered at all, is seen as strictly an internal management issue. But an "I'M FIRST" company will see this in a broader perspective, as being important to the customer—something that she will notice.

> **See the organization through the customer's eyes.**

While conducting a seminar for the top managers of a major Las Vegas resort/casino, I asked if they were truly in the hospitality industry. The answer was "No." They said they were selling escape, fantasy, and release from tension. They're not providing hotel rooms, they're fulfilling dreams. No wonder this resort ranks with the leaders in customer satisfaction among Las Vegas hotels! They know what the customer seeks, and every employee is trained to understand this and act accordingly— among themselves as well as toward their customers.

Your management also must see things in a broad perspective and make that vision part of the company's framework, so that *employees see their purpose as greater than the specific tasks they are hired to do.*

At the training seminars I present for my clients, I ask

participants to introduce themselves and tell what they do. Invariably, they give their job titles. I reply, "OK, your *title* is such-and-such in the so-and-so department. But what do you *do?*"

Then they describe their jobs as a *process:*

- "I get these forms from Jane, check to see that all the blanks are filled in, add up the columns, then give them to Harry."
- "I coordinate three people's work and make sure that the project is staying on schedule."
- "I review engineering plans to see that they conform to the City Building Code."

Then I ask everyone to complete this sentence: "As a result of my coming to work in the morning, the customer benefits _____."

Ask your staff (and yourself) the "What do you do?" questions. How long does it take before they get to the word *customer?* Considering their jobs in light of how the customer benefits is invariably a revelation to many employees.

> **Help each employee see her job as a contribution to the organization's total impact on the customer.**

A final example of seeing your agency from the customer's point of view:

In his excellent book, *What They Don't Teach You at Harvard Business School,* Mark H. McCormack tells of having dinner with Andre Heiniger, chairman of Rolex. A friend came up to say hello to Heiniger and asked, "How's the watch business?"

"I have no idea," Heiniger replied.
His friend laughed. Here was the head of the world's

most prestigious watchmaker saying he didn't know what was going on in his own industry.

But Heiniger was deadly serious. "Rolex is not in the watch business," he continued. "We are in the *luxury* business."*

Herr Heiniger knows what business is about. He's not selling watches, he's selling a lifestyle.

What are *you* selling? Write down a few answers to that question until you get to the broadest possible one. Start with the shoes you manufacture, then work your way out to warmth, comfort, style, self-image. What is it that the customer is really buying? How can your offices, sales force, receptionists, and plant workers look/act/dress/respond in order to become a positive, contributing part of that vision?

Sustaining Employee Pride

Sally Reed looks at me intently as we sit at a conference table enjoying the sunny California view from her office. She is chief executive of Santa Clara County. "Individual employees thrive on their ability to resist the public, instead of identifying with the public and trying to help them," says Reed. She is in the forefront of those fighting this resistance by applying the concept of customer service to government.

Reed was appointed county executive officer in the famous Silicon Valley in 1981 and now employs 14,000 people and oversees a budget of $1.4 billion per year. In recognition of her many achievements, she received a National Public Service Award from the American Society for Public Administration.

"I got to the issue of customer satisfaction from a very indirect route," Reed says. "Not so much because I was concerned about the customer—although it's true I was very con-

*From *What They Don't Teach You at Harvard Business School: Notes from a Street-Smart Executive*, by Mark H. McCormack, copyright © 1984 by Book Views, Inc. Reprinted by permission of Bantam Books, a division of Bantam, Doubleday, Dell Publishing Group, Inc.

cerned about courtesy and service—but one of the things that reinforced it for me was my emphasis on pride in public service, trying to make employees feel proud of what they do."

One way that she influences her employees' customer service decisions is by continually asking her top managers, "How will the move you're proposing improve customer service?" She provides special training to her employees to impart the service skills they need to be successful. Her views on customer service are widely known among county employees.

Why does she bother? After all, local government has a monopoly, so why should it care about customer service? If you need a building permit, you cannot go to the next City Hall down the road. No one else has a sale offering you better environmental quality at a more competitive price. And the next time you need a business license, you're going to go back to the same counter at City Hall, whether you got good service there the last time or not.

Well, the customer confronting today's City Hall knows what good service is. He's been to Nordstrom, he owns an IBM computer, he knows the consideration he deserves. This customer knows whether he feels good about dealing with local government. Increasingly, he does not. Citizen discontent has led to:

- Increasing numbers of revenue-limiting initiatives such as Proposition 13 and its successors in California
- Failed bond issues for roads and schools
- Complaints to the city council and to the city manager's office
- Supervisory personnel duplicating work that should be handled by public-contact personnel
- Loud and bitter objections to higher salaries for lawmakers and public officials
- Public-contact staff members (who usually see themselves as underpaid and who frequently work in antiquated of-

fices) becoming unnecessarily frustrated, tense, mortified, and feeling helpless about their ability to do a good job— so they don't do a good job, or they quit and you have to hire and train someone new

Beyond these problems, services traditionally performed by government, such as trash collection, park maintenance, and even fire protection, are being contracted out to private agencies. The thinking is that "government will only mess it up," that "dining at the public trough" makes a person lazy and uncaring, and that civic workers are not good enough to get a job in private business.

This wounds the reputation and limits the future of local government and the people who make it work. The "best and the brightest" will avoid government jobs. Sally Reed is fighting this trend by using the integration concept. Reed told me that many people in her community work for Hewlett-Packard, a computer manufacturer known for its progressive personnel policies.

People like H-P and enjoy working there, Reed says. When you meet one of them at a party, they invariably will talk about how great it is to work at H-P, how excited they are about what they're doing, how the supervisors give them plenty of freedom to approach problems, and on and on. Reed wants the county to have that image.

Whether it be the public or the private sector, an integrated customer service orientation combining all of the "I'M FIRST" principles will create that kind of pride.

Goal: Powerful Problem-Solving, Not Perfection

When customer service is the prevailing value system in your organization, people understand and accept the role they play in the problem as well as in the solution. Thus, they can spring into action and turn a problem into an opportunity.

Security Pacific Corporation is the nation's seventh-largest bank holding company, with 43,000 employees. Security Pacific

Automation Company, Inc. (SPAC) is its data processing and operations arm. Among other things, it provides advanced technological systems for Security Pacific worldwide. John Singleton is chairman, president, and chief executive officer of SPAC, and vice-chairman of Security Pacific Corporation.

Although I had been working with Security Pacific Corporation and SPAC for a few years, and had been very impressed with how they are managed, I first met with Singleton in November 1986, in his luxurious fifty-fourth-floor executive office at Security Pacific's international headquarters in downtown Los Angeles.

While a uniformed security officer guarded the entrance to his executive suite, Singleton (despite a troublesome back ailment) got down on his hands and knees to find a convenient electrical outlet for my tape recorder. Throughout our conversation, he frequently adjusted the heavy draperies to shield my eyes from the sun. What a disarming study in contrasts!

Singleton talked to me about his company's excellent reputation for service and integrity. His story:

We had a senior executive who drove us nuts about complaints. He would get customer complaints and he would always write a letter zinging us. We decided that every time a problem came up, we would send a backup memo: "Here's what we've done." "Here's another two-week follow-up on what we've done."

Finally, he called me one day and said, "I will never send you another memo. Stop the follow-up memos and calls. Please, call your people off!"

We broke up in hysterics laughing over that. We killed him with service! He said, "If you're doing all these things, and I gather you are because I've talked to some of these customers, I don't need to send you any more of these memos." So we took a person who was our worst critic and turned him around because we made him forget the problem. We said, "We're always going to have problems. You can send us a note every week. You know we handle thousands and millions of transactions. But when we have a problem, we fix it better than anybody else around."

You see, that's the thing that people miss. They say, "Don't have problems." *You cannot legislate problems out of existence. What you can do is fix them better than anybody else around.*

That's what we say to our personnel. "You will fix problems better than anybody else—with the right attitude, the right follow-up, and the right tenacity."

Your customer will remember the *satisfying outcome,* not the original error.

Management's job is to have employees understand that individual shortcomings, occasional haphazard work, product failure, or slow mail delivery are part of the human condition and will be forgiven—if they are built on an institutional history of positive customer relationships. But negative people interaction, in contrast, is rarely forgiven by the customer.

A landmark study conducted for Coca-Cola Company by Technical Assistance Research Programs is detailed in Warren Blanding's book, *Practical Handbook of Distribution and Customer Service.**

This study, Blanding notes, "established conclusively that consumers who felt well-disposed toward the firm after making an initial complaint tended to significantly increase their consumption of Coca-Cola, while those who were less pleased showed a marked decline in their purchases of the soft drink. Other studies have shown that loss of customer goodwill results in partial or complete loss of business; consultant Harvey Shycon quantified the cost at *$20,000 per incident* [emphasis mine] as long ago as 1973."

---

*Published by International Thomson Transport Press (Washington, D.C.), 1985. The quote that follows is reprinted with the publisher's permission.

In a well-run company, the number of absolute catastrophes is going to be small. What can kill a company, however, is the long-term, cumulative effect of a series of small problems or situations that are mishandled. With the "I'M FIRST" system, effective employee response to a problem becomes automatic. The hit-or-miss method of problem-solving is eradicated. You are in control in a whole new way.

Get Credit for How Good You Are

As Singleton did with his complaining executive, you must be sure that the customer *knows* that he is getting something special. As part of integration, employees need to know how to call the customer's attention to their good work.

IBM taught me this while I was deputy chief administrator of San Diego County, California. Two of the fourteen departments I supervised were data processing and the registrar of voters. Very early in my tenure, the county decided to buy an electronic rapid vote-counting system. (The votes had been tabulated previously by hand-feeding individual ballots into an optical scanner.)

In the conversion process, we worked with two major vendors. One sold us the vote-counting software package. Because the vote-counting process used our existing IBM mainframe, the other vendor was International Business Machines. We were all very nervous about what we were doing because the first real test of the new system was a major election: the June 1980 statewide primary. Many eyes in the state—and in the nation—were watching to see if we could pull it off.

As I recall, a few days before Election Day, I received a telephone call from IBM. "Ms. Goldzimer, we're flying two of our experts to San Diego and they will be with your staff through Election Day." The next day, I was visited by my IBM account representative: "Linda, I want to review with you all of our systems checklists. We're very confident—and you should be, too—that everything is going to work fine."

On the Monday morning before Election Day, I received another phone call from IBM: "Linda, I want you to know that we now have, in the basement with your IBM mainframe, three IBM technicians. They will sleep there tonight.

"And they will sleep there Election Night. Nothing will go wrong. However, I want you to know they will be there just in case a problem arises."

The software vendor essentially did the same thing. That vendor flew in experts from other parts of the country. That vendor had personnel working in the registrar's office for days on end, testing and retesting the system.

But they never told me about it. Guess who made the better impression on me—the customer: IBM. IBM's people not only provided fabulous service, but they made certain that their customer *knew* she was getting fabulous service.

Let's say your employees stayed very late one night last week to handle a customer's request, or your staff personally delivered some documents because the normal distribution network wasn't quick enough, or you did extra research and preparation to guarantee a fail-safe implementation of the customer's new system.

What subtle methods can you use to make certain that your customer knows about these special efforts? Draw a line down the center of a sheet of paper. In the left column, list everything "special" that you did for a customer during the last month. In the right column, write down how and when you will gently remind the customer of how good you are! How can you integrate this kind of self-credentialing into your employees' daily interactions with customers? Your customers cannot appreciate and value what they do not know about. Fixing a record of your good efforts in their minds is a pathway to repeat business.

Your Employees as the Customers' Advocates

Here is a vivid illustration of the thinking that comes with integration:

"The sale only happens once. [Then] the long-term relationship with the customer becomes the critical factor in staying competitive," said Lawrence Sills of Standard Motor Products. "If you ask anybody in our industry who has the best sales force, they'll tell you it's Standard. But if you ask each salesperson what his job is, their real job is not just to make the sale. *Their real job is to look after the customer.* In fact, that's their only job.

"We check [the customer's] inventory, we check their catalogues, we check their price sheets, check their defective merchandise, train their counter people, work their promotions—in fact, some would say we actually do their job for them.

"Our whole purpose is to develop a long-term relationship between the salesperson and the customer. Each salesperson is viewed as the customer's advocate within the company. Our customers see them that way, and that is how each salesperson is viewed by the home office."

At Standard Motor Products, the salespeople become representatives of the customer instead of representatives of the company. Since Standard controls 30 percent of the market he supplies in auto replacement parts, you have to figure that they're doing something right.

Sills' salespeople are truly working *for* their customers. The implication is that they will fight *against* the company if their customer needs something badly. Integration carries through to Standard's home office personnel, who recognize the sales force's role as the customers' advocates, supporting and actually enforcing a policy of "looking after" the customer.

That is what I'm after with my clients, and what you can achieve, starting with integration. Your employees must see their link to the customer, even if they never talk to a customer. They must know that their best effort is the only one that's acceptable. From bottom to top, everyone in your organization should have an identical approach to customer service: a positive, "no-problem" advocacy of the customer's point of view.

My integration concept fits into *your* business, whether it's a medical office, a shoe factory, a private school, a city transit department, a stationery store, or your own entrepreneurship.

The power wielded by a group of people fixed on a common purpose is one of the most under-utilized powers that companies have—and it has the potential to create tidal waves of productivity and sales.

Using integration, you will have this power.

3

Management with a Mission

*"In normal times, followers create leaders.
In times of crisis, choose FDR or Lincoln.
In between, choose what's his name."*
—AUTHOR UNKNOWN

Let's open our discussion of management with a mission by asking a few questions. Jot down your responses. After you have completed this chapter, review your answers. You will easily see what you most need to do to make your agency a customer-driven one.

- How many long-term corporate goals have you set?
- Do you treat your employees as you would want your external customers to be treated?
- What are the most powerful competitive pressures facing your company?
- How would your staff evaluate your organization?
- What is the force that governs your organization: the whim of the marketplace, strict application of company policies, or the demands of the customer?
- How many people in your company are involved in customer service?
- Who are your customers?
- How do you deal with employees who oppose your plans?
- What priority does customer service *really* have in your company?

- Does management accept its responsibility for customer satisfaction?

Choose Your Goals Carefully—You May Achieve Them

That hoary advice is repeated so often because it is true. If you strive to be adequate, that's what you'll be. The key is to know how to be exceptional. Set higher standards. Shoot for loftier goals.

Sally Reed, county executive officer for Santa Clara County, California, recommends and follows the goal-setting philosophy found in *Memorandum for the president—Strategic Approach to Domestic Affairs in the 1980s*, written for President Jimmy Carter by Benjamin W. Heineman, Jr., and Curtiss A. Hessler (New York: Random House, 1980). The authors hold that a president will be able to accomplish only three or four things while in office. Reed says the book "legitimized the fact that that's all that any of us does in jobs like this. So I have chosen a handful of things I want to accomplish, and I literally incorporate them in every single thing I do."

With such a short list of possible accomplishments, each manager must choose his or her goals very carefully. Take a moment now to write down your top priorities. Then answer these questions:

- What goal will have the greatest leverage in my organization?
- What will benefit my organization most—in the long run?
- How can I help shape my company so that it is recognized as a leader in its field and customers will return to us again and again?

Try Washing the Windows

When he took over the Metro-North Commuter Railroad, which serves New York City and its Connecticut suburbs, in

1983, "service was terrible, and no one believed it would ever get better," Peter Stangl told me.

"It was essential that we gain some credibility with: one, our customers; two, the elected officials who vote tax dollars for us; three, my board of directors. And four, ourselves.

"I wanted to pick a couple of things that I knew people didn't believe would ever get better, to improve credibility with all four of those groups."

What four goals did he select?

- Getting the morning trains to run on time
- Getting the air conditioning in the train cars to work properly
- Washing the train windows
- Having the conductors be courteous

And that's it.

"Let's get our customers to work on time," Stangl decided. "If we could do that, the evening rush hour would take care of itself eventually.

"When you take over an operation like this, you need to buy some time for yourself. I also thought that, in the long run, the most important thing was having employees of this railroad have some confidence in themselves, to believe in themselves."

By concentrating on those four goals—which had high visibility to his customers and enhanced his employees' self-esteem—Stangl was able to effect positive momentum that in time would help expand his base of achievable goals.

What does your organization do to enhance morale and customer service? Figuratively speaking, are the windows of your train cars dirty? Make it your mission to keep them clean.

"The increasing emphasis on serving the customer . . . suggests that the most successful companies of the future will be those that best move *as a total entity* [emphasis mine] to meet their customers' needs," says Warren Blanding in his *Practical Handbook of Distribution and Customer Service* (Washington, D.C.: International Thomson Transport Press, 1985).

A rule of thumb he cites states that the cost of a lost customer is the equivalent of about five years' worth of sales to that customer. In other words, the loss of a customer billing $100,000 a year and showing a 10 percent account growth rate would represent a total loss of roughly $610,000.

Fascination with the quick buck to be made from corporate takeovers, added to the customary emphasis on quarterly or annual gains, has left many U.S. companies without a long-term focus and plan as they fight for every dollar with foreign and domestic competitors. Businesses may know how to win in the short term but not how to *repeat their* success. Having a *long-term mission* helps you create systems that will succeed today, tomorrow, and far down the road. This commitment must come from the top executives. Your objective must be to gain new customers and to keep them. Every decision must be measured against that imperative.

Or, as nationally known professional speaker Ira Hayes is fond of saying about the masterpiece presentation that he has performed for years to the delight of thousands: "Anyone can give a great speech one time, but try to give it a thousand times, fella!"

Pick a *few* corporate goals.
Have a plan for now *and* the future.
Relate these goals to the customer.

Here's how you can sustain consistent first-rate performance.

Five Steps to Managing with a Mission

1. Recognize that good customer service can happen only within a healthy organization.
2. Examine your competitive environment and set your goals accordingly.

3. Survey your employees—take a picture of their outlook.
4. Establish who's in charge: the rules or *you*?
5. Get everyone involved, so everyone has a vested interest in achieving your goals.

How to Achieve Your Mission: Step 1

Recognize that good customer service can happen only within a healthy organization.

William B. Kolender, former chief of the San Diego Police Department, has brains, charm, wit, energy, leadership, and political savvy that sustained him as chief of police in the seventh-largest city in the country for fourteen years. He also has served on the executive board of the International Association of Chiefs of Police and was chairman of the United States Major City Police Chiefs.

At the time he resigned in July 1988, Kolender's years as chief of the San Diego PD made him the longest-tenured big-city police chief in the country. Kolender is now working in the private sector as assistant general manager for the Copley Press, a San Diego–based newspaper chain.

The San Diego Police Department, with less than two officers for every thousand citizens, accomplishes a job that takes other police departments twice as many people to do. How did Kolender create and sustain such effectiveness?

"The relationship that . . . any public agency has with the people . . . *starts from within,* not from without," Kolender said. "[It shows in] the way in which managers deal with their people, the way they care for their staff. By that I mean . . . a concern for their environment, for their family life, for each employee as a person. . . .

"I also mean, by caring, that you are willing to assist in the development of goals. You are willing to give direction, you are willing to hold [people] accountable. To me, that's a part of . . . letting people know that you care about them. . . ."

So it isn't simply warm feelings and hand-holding.

"I think most people will do what the boss wants them to do," Kolender continues. "Too many bosses don't have the chutzpah to tell them what to do. People like to know where they stand. They like to know what's expected of them. And I've never heard anybody complain about being held accountable as long as they thought it was fair. Not ever. And I've been around here a long time.

"Once you have developed a humanistic approach toward your people, I think they can take that into the community."

> Your employees will relate to your customers the same way that you and your managers relate to them.

"The staff will absorb the mentality of management," agrees Mario Arrigo, general manager of the classic five-star Villa d'Este on Lake Como, Italy.

General Manager David Semadeni of the Brazilian Court Hotel, a lovely four-star hotel in Palm Beach, Florida, states that the staff is the "translation between the customer and the hotel."

That is true in any work situation. Your staff is constantly conveying your ideas, policies, and products to your customers. If they do not know their mission and feel good about themselves, their company, and the product, you can be sure that your customers won't, either. Suzanne Foucault, former city manager of Oceanside, California, put it this way: "Your employees cannot be positive across the counter if they don't feel positive about what is going on on their side of the counter."

As a former public employee, I can vividly recall the pain I felt whenever I was embarrassed by an elected official in a public meeting—frequently before TV cameras, radio microphones, and newspaper reporters. That was when I concluded that it takes a saint to treat the customers gently after you have been roughed up by your boss.

So you have to show your employees that you care. Caring means clearly telling each employee what you expect, creating the conditions that allow them to deliver what you want, and holding them accountable for their actions.

When he first assumed office, Chief Kolender said, "I did some things to let the officers know that I care.

"It used to be [that on] October first every cop had to put on a long-sleeved shirt. Well, it might be ninety-five degrees that day. I said, 'Wait a minute, my officers have enough brains to know if it's cold or hot!'"

He also let them take off their hats. "And then people identified with them, and the cops loved it."

These were simple matters, but they touched the officers' lives directly and let them know that management cared about their personal comfort.

This story from Peter Stangl of Metro-North railroad demonstrates how discipline and maintaining order—fairly and evenly—within the organization shows that management cares, while still enforcing its goals:

"When we took over the railroad, I don't think anyone was holding anybody accountable for anything. . . . In certain cases people didn't even know to whom they reported.

"So we firmed up the organization and we fired some people. We hired some different people. We promoted some people from within.

"And we began to focus hard—and fairly, I think—on discipline. For example, we found fifteen or twenty people sloughing off—I mean they were asleep or they had disappeared from their jobs—and we brought them all in on charges, including the foremen."

Stangl continued: "Now, that's the time I got a call from [a union official concerning] the foremen, saying, 'Why are you bringing my people in? They didn't do anything wrong.'

"To which I responded, 'They're the managers of [their] group.' The union official replied, 'Yeah, well, they are, they're the foremen.' I said, 'Well, if I can't hold them accountable for what the people reporting to them do, then I don't need the foremen.'

"And it's really that simple. I don't care whether you are unionized or not: If you're supervising people, you're going to be held accountable for the people who work for you. . . If the quantity of work or the quality of work is no good or if people are stealing time from the company, we're going after those employees, and we're going after the person who manages them."

That's how a leader with a mission begins to refocus his or her organization. A customer-driven organization is not haphazard. It is highly disciplined. It is an organization where all the employees, *whether or not they have direct customer contact*, know that you care about them and what they do, and that they are held responsible for extending that caring to the customer.

A caring organization is also a disciplined one.

How to Achieve Your Mission: Step 2

Examine your competitive environment and set your goals accordingly.

To guide your company into the next century, you must examine the external environment in which your customer relationships exist. Consider these factors:

• *Technological changes.* You can look at these in two ways: administrative and integral. New administrative tools include facsimile machines, memory telephones to speed calls, word processors, pagers, and cellular telephones. All of these can improve your employees' productivity.

Examples of integral technology are the evolution of medical diagnostic tools and computer-assisted manufacturing. If you're a doctor and you've just learned how to operate an X-ray machine, you're way behind. Sonograms and CAT scans are replacing X-rays in many cases because they're seen as less intrusive to the patient—while allowing the physician to see more of the patient. Tomorrow, magnetic resonance imaging may supplant all of these as ways to peer inside people.

In the field of color printing, a $1,500 tool called a densitometer measures the intensity of each color that the presses print on the page. This can save thousands of dollars over the wasteful system of comparing the product to the original, then guesstimating how to turn brown into blue while the presses are rolling.

Look for innovative applications of technology to your business. Your competitors will!

• *Transportation and communications.* Overnight delivery systems—Purolator, Federal Express, United Parcel Service, Emery, even Uncle Sam's—have allowed firms to serve wider markets and in some cases have created new ones. On the coast of central and southern California, abalone farming is a growing enterprise that couldn't have existed five years ago. Quicker transportation allows producers to keep the tasty morsels fresh for diners at fine restaurants throughout the Southwest.

As roads become more and more congested, consider ways to transport employees more efficiently by subsidizing monthly bus passes, organizing car pools, or letting more people work at home with computer link-ups.

In communications, satellites are gaining wider and wider commercial use. The Automotive Satellite Television Network videotapes instructional programs for broadcast to its 2,500 member dealerships nationwide. By the time you read this, I will have videotaped five programs for the subscription network, giving me a much wider audience for those training sessions than I could reach in person.

Video and telephone technology combine to produce video conference calls, allowing your Denver staff to meet face to face with your customer's Milwaukee staff in the morning—and they can all spend a productive afternoon in their own offices.

What new tools will you be able to employ in the future?

What creative uses can you find for existing means of transportation and communications?

• *Legislation and the consumer movement.* Congress rewrote the entire federal tax code in 1986, then modified that in 1987. It's a safe bet that more "fine-tuning" will be done in the 1990s.

Another factor on the legislative front is the increasing strength of consumer protection and product liability laws. (It has been said that the U.S. Food and Drug Administration wouldn't allow the marketing of *aspirin* if a pharmaceutical firm proposed it today, because scientists can't show how it works!)

Insurance costs have risen to the point where city governments, for example, are creating their own pools of insurance monies and dropping their coverage with traditional carriers. State and federal governments are beginning to investigate this problem—as are the insurance companies.

These are examples of the regulatory situation in two industries. What changes in tax and consumer laws are on the horizon for your business?

• *Political environment.* Is the government's policy laissez-faire, stressing local and state control? Or is it a permissive, free-spending one with subsidies for business and individuals? (I'm offering no predictions here, just the possibilities.) Does the future hold tariffs and protectionism or new rules to encourage imports? How can your firm take advantage of these policies? What foreign countries encourage investment? Which are politically unstable and should be avoided?

• *Social environment.* Sociologists tell us of the "graying of America" as people are living longer and healthier lives. The Sun Belt cities of the South and West are growing phenomenally. Teens and pre-teens have become significant sources of spending power. Workers are opting for more flexible hours and more leisure time. With today's two-income families, executives are less willing to move for the convenience of the conglomerate unless two jobs are offered.

Is your firm prepared to respond to these demographic changes? What are your competitors doing?

• *Economic environment.* Inflation or disinflation? Rising or falling interest rates? Good times or bad times, there's money to be made. You've got to keep a close eye on the overall economy and stay abreast of trends and expectations.

All of these factors have direct impact on your customers and employees. As your firm's leader, you need to identify these conditions and turn them to your benefit. Keep yourself informed. Look for trends, using varied sources of information. Read *Forbes* and the *Wall Street Journal,* sure. But don't neglect *Rolling Stone* or the newsletter of the American Association of Retired Persons. You need to see the whole spectrum of ideas in order to formulate the right goals.

How to Achieve Your Mission: Step 3

Survey your employees—take a picture of their outlook.

Your organization is an interdependent organism, even though it may be divided into operating units and departments. Ultimately, these branches depend on one another. Your mission is to learn what is helping or hindering your employees from making the organization customer-driven. Let's look at the agency from your employees' point of view.

Below is a list of questions that will measure your organization's progress toward becoming customer-driven. After writing down your answers to these questions, conduct a survey of your employees and compare your answers to theirs.

• What is quality service?
• Are we organized to encourage quality service?
• Do you perceive customer service as an important value?
• Do you understand what you are supposed to achieve on the job? And with each customer?
• Are you held accountable for the quality of service that you give?
• Do you have the training you need to perform effectively?

- Do you feel that you can take extra time on the job to work with customers?
- Are you rewarded appropriately for your work with customers?
- Do you receive constructive feedback to help you perform more effectively?
- How well are we cooperating internally? Do we treat each other as customers?
- Do you have the authority you need to solve customer problems? If not, what would be helpful?
- Do you have enough say in formulating company policy on dealing with your customers?
- How good are our internal communications? (That includes the telephone system, employees' ability to avoid misunderstandings, effectiveness in getting the word out on policies, even the delivery of inter-office mail.)

Now, there are many different ways to uncover this and other vital information. One is to glean the information as perceived (and filtered) by others—from their memos, reports, and data printouts. Another way to get information is to go into the plant, stop by people's offices, eat in the company cafeteria, and ask the questions yourself.

These methods have value and should be utilized. They uncover what Paul Sanchez, a director of communications and survey operations for Wyatt Company, a forty-five-year-old "full-service human resource consulting firm," calls the "emotional texture" of the agency. But they should be coupled with an employee survey designed to give you the objective data you need, efficiently and in a useful format.

Opening a Dialogue: The Employee Survey

By surveying your managers' and employees' opinions, you are opening a dialogue with the important people who translate your ideas to your customers. Here are six crucial guidelines.

1. Your survey must have very specific objectives. Phrase your questions to give you the data you need. The data you collect will be only as good as the questions you ask. Watch out for the "nice-to-knows." Stick to the "need-to-knows," as in the list above.

2. The questions should be grouped into "manageable and related chunks," Sanchez says.

Examples of "chunks" are:

The mental environment, culture, or value system of the organization.

The physical environment—lighting, cleanliness, roominess, ventilation.

The management environment. Does it work?

The communications environment. In dealing with your customers, vendors, suppliers, shareholders, other employees, the media, and so on, do people have the information they need, in the right form at the right time?

Goal orientation. What is the focus of your company? Is there a plan so that people know what role they play in serving the customer?

3. Confidentiality *must* be observed. Employees must believe that their answers and identities will be protected; otherwise, the replies are less honest. You want unadulterated facts. Therefore, responses should be anonymous.

4. When you talk to employees about the survey, make it very clear that this is not a witchhunt; the goal is to make the entire organization more effective.

5. Supervisors must feel comfortable with the survey and understand that they will not be undermined by the results. Bring them in at the beginning of the process. Find out what questions *they* want to ask. What is *their* opinion of the questions that others want to ask? Union leaders and members also should be part of the process.

"If the union is excluded," Sanchez says, "they will tell the workers, 'Don't fill out the survey,' 'If you do fill it out, fill it out wrong, or give biased answers.'"

Generally, Sanchez says, union leaders will be cooperative. When presented to union leaders as an attempt to "make this a better place to work," the survey becomes acceptable. Management should say to the union, "Please pass the word that it's OK to fill out the forms." Ask the union leaders to announce it in their newsletter and to post related announcements on their bulletin boards. This gives the union a stake in the survey's success. The union leaders may not endorse the survey, but you should work to see that they do not oppose it.

6. Don't surprise anyone with this survey. Approximately a month ahead of time, begin to talk about the survey and what it will measure.

A sample employee survey, conducted by the *Los Angeles Times* in 1987, is in Appendix 2. The *Times*' goals for its survey may differ from yours. But the overall form is a good guide.

So now you have formulated specific objectives for your survey. You have involved your supervisors and union leaders. You have communicated well and often about the survey project, so no one is surprised. Now your results are in. What happens next?

"Remember, you have started a dialogue," Sanchez says. "It's just like being polite. It is as if the top executive walks up to you and says, 'Hi, how are you?' [And] you respond, 'Gee, I've got a cold and a headache today.' But the boss turns on his heel and walks away. You are left with your mouth open," recognizing that he doesn't really care.

Get back to the staff quickly with the results of the survey and *act* on them! As Sanchez says, "Organizations that don't do anything with the results will poison the well for many, many years—as long as the memory of the employees lasts."

Sanchez tells of a survey he did for a utility company. "A lady who was a thirty-year employee walked to the front of the room and slapped the survey back down on the table," he said. "She said she wasn't going to take it because the last time she took a survey, which was something like 1958, she never heard anything about it. She wasn't going to waste her time doing it again."

Your organization should clearly identify the changes that result from survey data. That way, employees see that the survey is indeed a dialogue with top management—and that management is listening.

> **To transform your firm into a customer-driven company, first take an accurate picture of how it really operates.**

How to Achieve Your Mission: Step 4

Establish who's in charge: the rules or you?

In chapter 1, we talked about the evolution of business from being product-driven to market-driven to customer-driven. There is a fourth type of organization that, while it may combine aspects of the first two, has taken on a separate identity because of its unique emphasis on policy.

I describe this kind of company as *organizationally* driven. Management writes its definitions of efficiency and effectiveness based on suppositions, not surveys. The bureaucracy is so entrenched that nothing can shake it. "Because we've *always* done it this way" is the answer to a new employee's "Why?"

In an organizationally run company, policies and procedures dictate how the customer is handled. Examples:

- "You must wait five days before you can use your credit card."
- "We deliver between eight and ten A.M.—no exceptions. And we make no appointments."
- "There are no exchanges after seven days."
- "You must have your service contract and your original two-inch by half-inch sales slip to get a credit."

Detroit spends millions every year smashing cars into walls, running them for hundreds of thousands of miles at high speeds, and baking the paint—all to test the quality of their product. They warranty it and guarantee it. They'll even loan you the money to buy it. Other industries test the quality of the service they provide by asking questions such as "Was the repairman polite?" "Was the room clean?" "Was the technician able to answer your questions?"

Both of these "testing" methods are necessary. However, *few organizations realize how often they and their customers are captives of their own rules.*

Clumsy or seemingly arbitrary rules can, and frequently do, sabotage the best market offerings.

In addition to testing the quality of the product or service you are selling, test the quality of your rules.

Try these two exercises:

• Ask your customer-contact workers, "What rule or policy prevents you from satisfying the customer?" If the same rule pops up frequently, you need to reevaluate that rule. Don't expect the customers to change (they won't). The rule should be updated, modified, or eliminated.

• Ask every employee in your company to state *how the customer benefits* from each company policy. If she cannot explain the benefit, either she needs to be better trained (see chapter 8), or the policy needs to be revised or buried.

Entrepreneur Ed Etess gives these three examples of rules that sabotage sales:

• "I stopped shopping at Montgomery Ward ten years ago because I couldn't get a catalogue. Sears would always give me a free catalogue. Montgomery Ward said you can't get a catalogue until you buy something. I said I can't buy something 'cause I don't have a catalogue. So I never bought anything and I never got a catalogue."

• "You get people who are administrators, the rulemakers. They say, 'You should do this,' 'You should do that.' 'If it's five P.M., it's time to shut off the lights, and if the customer is still there, too bad. He's got to leave.'"

• Top management must guard against "the accounting people, or the financial people, who are trying to drive up short-term profitability. They will make up rules such as 'You don't have any time as a serviceman to give advice to customers.'"

Contrast these two retailers' policies:

When a shopper returns an item at Sears, the receiving *store* is debited for the return. Each store, therefore, may be reluctant to accept a return of merchandise bought at another Sears location, because returns cut into its profit margin.

At Nordstrom department stores, anybody can return anything, anyplace in the store, at any store, at any time. Nordstrom makes you feel as good about returning something as you did about buying it. Moreover, the *salesperson* who originally sold the returned merchandise is debited for the return. This makes the *seller directly responsible* for the customer's satisfaction. She will work to avoid selling items that the customer really doesn't want or need. This kind of accountability keeps the customer foremost, and gives the salesperson a personal stake in making every sale a *final* sale.

Don't give up customer service to make life easier for your bureaucrats.

What's Right, Not Who's Right

"A manager should encourage all the employees to stop thinking about *who's* right or wrong and consider *what* is right or wrong," advises Joe Turner, senior vice-president of human resources of Home Federal Savings & Loan. "We try to get employees to think in terms of alternatives."

When faced with an irate customer or a difficult decision, it is quite natural for your staffers to become defensive and want to be "right." The rules then become a convenient way of asserting, "I'm right."

We know that the customer may not always be correct. Some customers can be very difficult. Some will cheat. Some will lie. Rulemakers establish procedures that hamper *every* transaction so they can protect the company from these abusive *few*. Guard against this.

For example, while most department stores (and many smaller stores as well) have adopted the use of security sensors attached to clothing in such a determined way that removal of the tag will make it a two-piece garment, Nordstrom has resisted this practice. The clips are bulky, heavy, unsightly, and ruin the fit when the customer tries on the garment. Nordstrom's position is "These tags are offensive and insulting to the majority of our customers; we will not use them."

Another example: Suppose that the first ten blanks on your standard contract are filled in incorrectly by 80 percent of your customers. Do you blame your customers? Do you attach a list of rules and clarifications? Instead, ask: If 80 percent of our clients are confused by this contract, haven't we done a poor job of drawing up the form? Redesign the form.

At my company, we never assume the customer made a mistake. My attitude when things go awry is that we goofed. We go back to the drawing board; we rarely establish a new rule. Companies often unknowingly impose rules and procedures that restrict employees and unfairly penalize customers. The rules, not you, can end up running your organization. Too many rules will ruin it as well.

Make your company user-friendly. *You* **take charge, not the rules.**

How to Achieve Your Mission: Step 5

Get everyone involved, so everyone has a vested interest in achieving your goals.

In a customer-driven organization, everyone feels as if they *own* their job; they're not just renting it. It's the difference between working for $9.46 an hour and working for the company.

"It doesn't do any good if the top twenty people or the top ten are involved . . . and everybody [else] is a cheerleader on the side. We've got to get the other thirty-eight hundred employees involved with the top managers," said John Singleton, chief executive officer of Security Pacific Automation Company, Inc. His company used the slogan "You Make the Difference" to show each employee the importance of his or her job. Singleton also held an off-site management conference on this theme "with two hundred managers, five levels deep in the organization."

The purpose, Singleton said, was to move each employee "from being a spectator *to crossing that line to where they're involved.* I think it's my job and the job of the senior management team to provide that motivation and that incentive . . . and the example."

How do you get your staff, particularly the people who never see a customer, to feel a proprietary interest in the customer? Here are eight tips.

1. *Explain how each job has a chain-reaction effect on other staffers' ability to do their jobs and therefore, eventually, on the customer.* If the clerks lose a case file, the attorneys can't find what they've done for the clients. That means expensive time wasted reconstructing the file, and the possibility that the client's case will be weakened. You want the clerk to do her job for the client, not just for her boss.

2. *Include all non-customer-contact personnel in programs designed to reinforce the importance of making the customer feel good.* Issue T-shirts saying, "You Make the Difference" to the

production department. Assign them to conduct mini-tours of the department for small groups of customers at an open house.

3. *Include non-customer-contact personnel in incentive programs, giving them a piece of the reward for customer service improvements.* For example, support personnel should share in the bonus when the sales staff tops its goals. (For more about incentives, see chapter 6.)

4. *Make sure that everyone has the "big-picture" concept of their job.* Home Federal Savings & Loan, for example, teaches product knowledge to its mailroom clerks. Moreover, every employee at Home Federal signs a contract (see Appendix 3) entitled "It's Up to You." This contract, which is part of the employee's personnel file, is one of the first things a new employee encounters when he starts work. It declares "Home Federal's goals" as an employer. It then lists "employee goals, as an official representative." This section declares the employee's responsibility to the customer. The contract is signed by the employee and by the human resources director and marketing director of Home Federal. The contract sets the tone from the first day: "Hey, we're serious about customer service."

Every business can take steps like these. If you own a resort hotel or other entertainment facility, instruct your auditors to appreciate how their mistakes on a bill can ruin a weekend stay. And inform your chefs and dishwashers who is being served at the restaurant that night.

5. *Explain each employee's job in terms of the actual effect it has on the life of the customer.* "I went into . . . our major overhaul and maintenance facility, walked up to an electrician on the line, and basically asked him why he was doing that job; why was he there?" Peter Stangl, president and general manager of Metro-North Commuter Railroad, told me.

"The electrician told me that his boss had told him to go there. He had been told to fix the car and that's why he was there. I said, 'I understand that, but why are you here? Why are you doing this?'

"He responded, 'I'm an electrician, I fix cars. I fix electrical components, that's why I'm here.'

"After I led this individual through five or six more questions, he finally realized: He was there because *someone* obviously *needed* his services. We had customers somewhere out on the railroad who couldn't get where they wanted to go unless he did his job properly so that the service was reliable.

"I don't think most people come to work in the morning and say, 'Let's see, if I do my job properly, the customer out there or the constituent I'm serving will get a good product and they'll be happy and I'll feel good about that.' Most people just don't think that way.

"They tend to come in and rewire the motors or write their memorandum or mix the cement, and don't stop to think about the *link* between what they do and . . . the *experience* that the customer has, and the fact that the customer is actually paying his salary. It is this *linkage* that I think is important and that is worth building."

Stangl has a mission: He wants his employees to appreciate that if the trains don't run reliably, Daddy's going to miss his son's Little League game, Mommy won't get to work on time, and Grandma will be left waiting alone at the deserted bus station.

"I genuinely believe that you can get a pretty good product by just setting goals—setting very few goals, by the way—and making them very clear, asking people to manage *to* those goals, and holding them accountable," Stangl says. "But I don't think you get an *excellent* product unless you also change the culture and people begin to [see] the *link* between the customer and what they do."

> **Every employee must understand that his efforts affect the actual life experience of each customer.**

---

6. *Design as many jobs as possible to give the worker higher visibility to the customer.* Knock a hole in the kitchen wall so the

restaurant guests can see the chefs—and the chefs can see their customers. Let the mechanic and the car owner talk to each other directly, without the "service rep" as intermediary.

7. *Institute programs that instill pride in getting the job done.* At the Boca Raton Hotel and Club, Ted Kleisner would invite his employees and their families to the club for dinner. Mothers, fathers, sisters, wives, husbands, and children were served dinner by management on the Sunday after Thanksgiving every year.

Particularly at this hotel, "which is a private club besides, so that no one off the street just comes walking in here to have dinner," Kleisner said. "It tells the employees' families that they are important. . . . [A bellman] is important enough that his boss is pouring coffee for him and his wife and his children."

8. *Make it easy for each employee to assume responsibility for customer service.* John Singleton of Security Pacific Automation Company, Inc., (SPAC) operates this way: Each employee is told his or her responsibilities to the company, specifically including how to handle customer complaints. These written guidelines deal with everything from minor inconveniences to the customer to critical "show-stoppers." For each type of problem, the employee clearly understands:

- The time in which she must resolve it
- Procedures for how to resolve it
- Assurance of her authority to resolve it
- How far she can go before she has exceeded her authority

Singleton gave me an example: "A major hardware failure [occurs] that's affecting a lot of automated teller machines." SPAC employees have certain parameters showing what each can do to fix that problem.

"But when they get to two hours, that's it," Singleton said. "They can do anything they want up to that two-hour [limit]. If it goes beyond two hours, it is out of their hands and has escalated, because it means that whatever creative things they did didn't work. . . . At that point, you need more clout and you need more resources to fix it."

SPAC's plan includes providing each employee with the name and phone number of the next person to contact if the problem hasn't been resolved within the time limit. Applying the doctrine of what's right, not who's right, keeps the ego out of it. Taking responsibility for customer service includes asking for help when you need it.

There you have the five steps for managing with a mission. Let's talk now about how to maintain momentum for your mission.

Expand Your Idea of Who Your Customer Is

I have defined a customer as someone who, motivated by self-interest, can choose to purchase your product or take his business elsewhere. Is this external customer the only one who will benefit from your management with a mission? No! All the elements in your organization must service one another *as if each were an external customer*—bosses, peers, and subordinates alike. Why? Because they need each other to be successful and because the "I'M FIRST" system requires a consistent approach to personal relationships.

During a seminar I recently conducted for some very top-level narcotics agents, someone raised his hand and said to me, "I don't have any customers. My job is to locate and arrest dopers. Who in the hell is my customer? We even shoot some of our customers. McDonald's doesn't."

"He's never gonna make it," Chief Kolender said when I asked his opinion of this man's comments.

"In order to arrest 'those dopers,' he's going to have to build relationships with an awful lot of other people in the community—people who would cooperate with him—informants, witnesses, troubled citizens, employees.

"Even someone who violates the law—no matter how serious that law might be—has a right to be treated with human dignity."

Your staffers probably won't be dealing with law-breakers every day. But a basic respect for human dignity must permeate their relationships with coworkers, subordinates, distributors, managers in other departments, and wholesalers. These people deserve the same treatment as your customers.

The mission statement of Marriott Hotels recognizes this broad definition of the customer:

> The mission of Marriott Hotels is to provide lodging and related services in a manner that builds strong, lasting, and satisfying relationships with customers, employees, owners, shareholders, and the communities in which it operates.

Blair Sadler of Children's Hospital and Health Center in San Diego lists his customers as: patients and their families; the donors who support the hospital; government officials who vote funds for state health insurance (held by 44 percent of his patients); "the educated community at large" (who are sensitive to health needs); and the doctors, nurses, and other employees of the hospital and health center.

This outlook follows my principle of making your employees feel good about *their* side of the counter so they can transfer those feelings to the public side.

Overcoming Resistance to Your Mission

What does a leader do when she encounters the resistance of other managers and of employees who oppose working on customer relationships, arguing that the status quo is fine? "Why should we waste production time at staff meetings or training sessions?" they ask. "We are already the market leaders in our field." How do you react when employees refuse to treat one another like customers?

Ted Kleisner, currently head of the five-star Greenbrier resort, dealt with it this way: "I was twenty-four years old when I was assigned as manager of the Terrace Hilton in Cincinnati. . . . It was extremely difficult, and people really wanted to see me fall flat on my face.

"If I had gone in . . . and tried to pull strings, it would have been [disaster] for sure. I needed to get people on my side, to win them over. And there is only one way to do that: *Go out there and talk to them*.

"I had been told, 'Whatever you do, don't talk to _____. He has been there forever. He rules his roost; he doesn't talk to anyone.'

"So that's where I started. I went to him and said, 'That's what I was told about you and I want you to know that I need all the help I can get.'

"That's the kind of philosophy I have used in my entire career. You start off by just talking to all the people."

I'm not going to pretend that you can accomplish all your goals just by talking people into things. It is very difficult for some people to change, and others never will. Some staff members will require:

- Closer supervision
- Incentives and rewards designed to alter behavior
- Counseling
- Retraining and coaching
- Progressive discipline in the form of warnings, lost pay, or suspensions

For others (I hope it's only a few), it may be your job to tell them that they and the job are not a good match and that they should move on because the job isn't going to change.

John Singleton of Security Pacific Automation Company says that he now and then holds an "Abraham Lincoln staff meeting, which only I attend, and we vote on some of these issues. And the vote surprisingly goes my way."

Singleton said, "I think you're kidding yourself when you say that participative management works all the time, because it doesn't. There are times when . . . you reach the culture barrier [with an individual employee]. By the time you climb over that barrier, you will have lost momentum.

"So, when I see momentum going down, I say, 'This culture change is going to happen. It would be nice if you supported it, but it will happen.'"

> **Do not ignore obstacles. Deal with them directly. Improved service to the customer is non-negotiable.**

Setting Priorities: The Three Elements of Productivity

Some of you may be saying, "You have sold me on the 'I'M FIRST' process. But I am a very busy manager. Can I keep my employees focused toward customer service—especially when they see a conflict between their productivity level and the mission of serving the customer?" Or, "Can you give me a classic case study of a management with a customer service 'mission' that runs a caring, disciplined, accountable, successful company?"

The answer to both questions is yes; keep reading.

Time and again, my clients question whether there is a conflict between productivity and customer service. The employee knows that he must attend meetings, write reports, and make sales. He worries that any extended contact with a customer will detract from these duties.

This happens because people try to give their bosses what the bosses want. If the staff thinks that the boss wants a very positive fourth quarter, more reports, more forms, or other concrete evidence of accomplishment, that's what he will get.

Suddenly, however, this same boss is saying that he wants more responsiveness to the customer: The phone should be answered before three rings; the mail answered within forty-eight hours; and creative solutions found for individual customer complaints.

The staff is confused. What takes priority? Here's an example of how to clear up this confusion.

Ed Etess is a highly successful entrepreneur. To date, he has founded three firms. One was Monitor Technology (the number one maker of air pollution monitoring equipment). The second was Computer Entry Systems (doing $72 million in sales in fiscal 1987 by supplying "check-reading" machines to various industries). The third is Web Technology. It's a new company that manufactures semiconductor test equipment for high-reliability uses. "We expect that within several years we'll be number one in our business area," Ed said.

Etess and I were talking in his office, located in a north San Diego business park. The decor is sparse, reflecting Etess's engineering background more than his status as a successful entrepreneur.

"I was recently consulted by another company that had decided to let its managers go because the managers couldn't handle the priorities," Etess told me. "I said, 'Have you ever discussed with the managers what their priorities were?'

"They said, 'No.'

"I said, 'Why not?'

"'Well, we pay a manager $100,000 a year. Don't you think he ought to know what his priorities are?'"

This firm was going to fire a group of people because *they weren't doing things they had never been asked to do!* Top management knew what its priorities were, but the next group down the pyramid was forced to guess.

That won't happen in a customer-driven company, because the leader with a mission knows the three components of productivity:

- First she determines the *acceptable level of tangible productivity* (weekly number of billable hours, number of blood samples drawn, number of phone calls made, number of buildings inspected, number of accounts opened) and communicates this to the employee.
- Second, she informs each employee of the expected *quality of service* to each customer.
- Third, she explains how these tasks rank in *order of importance.*

"Let's say you're in charge of inventory," Etess said. "We don't just say to you, 'We want you to turn the inventory three times a year.' We also tell you how important the turnover is in comparison to other things for which you are responsible."

Etess tells a story about a company that was being run against the customers' best interest. A customer's equipment was down and he needed a spare part. But the priority for this firm's production department was to ship the next customer's $10,000 piece of equipment. Everything was geared for that. They had no time to make $50 spare parts.

"If it's something I'm involved with," Etess said, "I'll tell people that the highest priority is the customer whose equipment is down."

What about the employee who has a report due to you in three hours (and you *really* need that report for a presentation you are making to your boss in six hours) and a customer calls this employee with a very time-sensitive problem? What should this employee do? He won't know that the customer comes first unless you tell him.

> Be specific about your *goals,* your *priorities,* and their *acceptable level of achievement.* Then, any conflict between productivity and customer service will disappear.

A warning, however: Once you set the priority that customer service is number one, you must stick to your guns. "This attitude starts [at] the top," Etess said. "If the president of the company allows things to get through because it's the end of the month and he'll make more money by shipping the product, people will realize that *and that will become the way they operate.*"

But if the president insists on sending out only the best product possible, his employees will know that the priority is top performance and the best service to the customer—no slacking off.

This happened to Etess one end-of-the-month weekend. It was time to ship the goods or lose any chance of making a stated sales goal. The engineering and quality control people came to him and said, "The equipment just is not working right."

"And if you ship it," Etess said, "you can make your financial goals, but then you've shipped a problem.

"I've gone to the customer and said, 'Look, I'd rather be late and have it right.'

"And we absorbed the loss. . . ." So might you. But you'll keep that customer—and gain more besides—ensuring escalating, long-term success.

How to Do It Right: The Nordstrom Way

Wherever a Nordstrom department store opens, nearby hospitals soon declare that they want to be the Nordstrom of the medical industry. Neighboring banks announce that they want to be the Nordstrom of the financial industry.

Nordstrom has become a benchmark for customer service against which other businesses measure themselves. It is a highly disciplined, well-managed organization that cares for and about its employees. Customers leave Nordstrom feeling good.

How does Nordstrom do it? What does the customer see?

The customer sees Nordstrom employees who are committed to doing whatever the customer would like. Each sales associate is told to develop her own clientele. Management tells each sales associate that they should see themselves (and be seen by the customers) as a personal shopper.

The customer sees a group of employees with initiative and drive. That happens because management gives each employee enough leeway to solve the customer's problems creatively. The customer sees management that truly backs its front-line people, supporting almost any idea that will help the customer or conforms to the "MNS" theme, which is "Make Nordstrom Special." The customer sees a management principle in action that says one sure way to get fired at Nordstrom is to promise the customer something and then drop the ball.

When a new employee comes on board, she is given a "personal book." The store manager explains that each employee's personal book represents her income. In this book, she keeps track of her customers' names, telephone numbers, likes, dislikes, charge card numbers—anything and everything that will help her be a personal shopper for that customer.

New employees receive personalized business cards and an open account to send thank-you notes or flowers to customers. They are told, "It is your customer and your department. Figure out how to make the customer happy."

What the customer *doesn't* see is the amount of support and reward the sales force gets. He doesn't see how decentralized and close to the customer the merchandising and buying are. Or how Nordstrom stocks such an unusual variety and quantity of merchandise—about twice the amount of inventory as its competitors. (They have clothes with different collar sizes for women, and odd shoe sizes for everybody.)

In this organization, the pay is generous and the production expectations are very high. Each person's sales volume, by the *hour*, is posted on bulletin boards near the employee entrance to the store. This is an organization where individuals, departments, and regions are compared with one another according to the criteria that are most important: customer service and sales volume production. Yet this organization also stresses ethics: It will fire an employee who knowingly takes sales from another employee.

A Final Word about Mission

Nordstrom's organizational chart shows the board of directors at the bottom. The executives are just above them; then comes middle management. Above all the other employees are the salespeople who deal with customers directly.

But at the top of the official organizational chart of this highly successful retailing firm are the customers. From the board of directors to the loading docks, the boss at Nordstrom is . . . me.

At Nordstrom, "I'M FIRST."

4

Feedback

"Would you do business with you?"
—LINDA SILVERMAN GOLDZIMER

During his memorable presentation at a National Speakers Association convention, Joe Weldon, a professional speaker and management consultant, asked the audience, "How many people have ever been bitten by an elephant?"

Of course, no hands went up.

"How many people here have ever been bitten by a mosquito or a gnat?"

Many hands went up.

Weldon smiled and declared, "Of course. Elephants don't bite! It's the little things in life that will eat you alive."

Most businesses bleed to death rather than explode. The number of businesses that fail because of some mega-mistake or some gigantic problem is relatively low. The slow leak, the quiet hemorrhage, is what kills companies over time. They lose touch with their customers and can only wonder why as they watch sales and profits ooze away.

You can escape this slow but certain death by establishing a purposeful, multi-sourced customer feedback network. For starters, write down all the methods you now use to obtain feedback from your customers. At the end of the chapter, we'll take another look at this list and see how you can add to it.

Unless you solicit continual feedback, you may think that everything you do is correct ("Well, we've had no complaints") or that everything you do is wrong ("All we ever hear are complaints"). Probably, neither assessment is correct.

My dictionary defines feedback as information that tells you of "discrepancies between intended and actual operation." Every moment of the day, your firm is broadcasting a message that determines whether customers will decide to do business with you. Your message may be positive, negative, or boring. Is the message your customers are receiving the one you intended to send? The feedback network we're going to set up will give you the answer.

Seven Benefits of Feedback

1. *Feedback reveals your customer's current and future plans, and lets you customize your approach to meet those needs.* This is how you can bind your customer to you with "golden handcuffs."

Feedback allows you to design a more comprehensive package for your customers than merely selling an isolated product. You can *make yourself indispensable* by becoming involved with their product development, advertising, promotions, and packaging. Offer your customers a system of interdependent services. You may wind up helping with their inventory management, cash management, financial management, and other programs, making it too expensive for them to change suppliers. In effect, you have created golden handcuffs.

2. *Seeing your business from your customer's point of view allows you to answer the question "Would you do business with you?"*

Have you ever presented a problem anonymously to see how your company handled it? Try standing in line, unrecognized, and go through the process that your customers experience in doing business with you. How does it look, sound, and feel? If you were a customer, would you be pleased with the response your company gave?

So-called "secret guests" or "mystery shoppers" are frequently used by the hospitality, retail, and airline industries to test the quality of the product and service being provided. Have these people report directly to you on their impressions of the job you're doing.

3. *Feedback allows you to tailor your service levels so you enjoy maximum customer satisfaction at a minimum cost.*

Before the Garden Grove, California, Police Department engaged in a federally funded customer service survey, any request for service meant that a patrol car was sent to the scene. "Someone would call in and say that an auto had hit a little boy crossing the street. A patrol car would be dispatched. The next call might be about your son losing his bicycle," Captain Stanley Knee said. "We would send a car to that, too.

"Traditionally, police departments felt that, in order to maintain citizen satisfaction, we needed to respond quickly to *all* calls. But the [survey] showed us that that's *not* what the customers want.

"As a result of the data, we . . . prioritize how we respond to calls for service."

More serious incidents get a more immediate response. But, for a stolen bicycle, the report is taken over the phone.

"We've reduced by almost a third the number of instances in which an officer actually goes out to the scene and takes a report. And that is an enormous financial savings." With no decline in customer satisfaction!

4. *If you don't ask, you'll never know how you're doing— until it's too late.*

"Clients are very funny," said my friend Ira Gottfried, a vice-president at Coopers & Lybrand in Los Angeles. "You'll suddenly find that the work stops and you don't get any new work. You seldom know why. It's a very rare client who will let you know they are having a problem."

How does he deal with that?

"By staying in constant touch. I . . . will call the clients periodically even though I am not dealing with them on a regular basis. I'll take them out to lunch. I will play golf with them."

Does he feel that he gets accurate data that way—even when it's bad news?

"Oh, yes, if you ask them, you will always get an answer. It's just that the Christian ethic says you don't nail somebody; you just walk away."

5. *Feedback is magnified by the "Iceberg Factor," making it more critical than it originally appears.*

"One of the sure signs of a bad or declining relationship is the *absence of complaints from the customer*," Theodore Levitt has written in the *Harvard Business Review*. "Nobody is ever that satisfied, especially not over an extended period of time. The customer is either not being candid or is not being contacted."*
No news is not good news—it's apathy.

How much weight should you attach to negative feedback?

If *one* customer complains to an airline, there are usually *twenty-five* additional dissatisfied customers, according to *The Consumer Affairs Department: Organization and Function* (New York: The Conference Board, Inc., 1973).

Corroborating this finding, only *one in twenty* commercial customers actually registers a complaint when he is dissatisfied with customer service, the authors of *Ways to Handle Customer Complaints* assert. Each seemingly insignificant gripe, then, represents a far bigger pool of complaints, and an absence of complaints does not necessarily mean that your customers are satisfied. You just haven't heard from that twentieth person yet.

Another way to see it: For every five complaints received, there are a hundred problem products out there. The scenario gets even more discouraging when you realize that, according to

*Reprinted by permission of the *Harvard Business Review*. Excerpt from "After the Sale Is Over," Theodore Levitt (September/October 1983). Copyright © by the President and Fellows of Harvard College. Used by permission. All rights reserved.

Ways to Handle Customer Complaints, the dissatisfied customer will tell eleven others, while the satisfied customer will tell just three others. This means that, for those hundred problems mentioned above, 1,100 people are hearing that your product is no good. From your original five complaints, the number of people who are hearing about what a crummy company you are has now been multiplied by 220! I call this phenomenon the *Iceberg Factor* because the complaints you receive are just a fraction of the problem, the tip of the iceberg.

I hope by now you're convinced of the titanic importance of *each and every* complaint.

6. *Feedback reveals what your competitors are doing, helping you to be a consistently strong contender.* As you spend time with your customers, you can pick up valuable information about trends in the industry, important personnel changes your customer is making, what your competitors are planning, new products on the market, and ways to expand your business to reach new markets. An effective ongoing customer feedback system can tell you what your competition is doing and what its image is among your customers and potential customers.

With this information, you can:

- Gear your cost/service mix toward areas in which you really do have to compete
- Avoid service levels that will raise your prices so high that you're non-competitive
- Eliminate services that don't matter to your customers
- Reject service levels that will not substantially differentiate you in the marketplace
- Fight off the competition

"We heard that our competitors were being solicited to replace us [in serving] a longtime client. We heard it on the street," a seasoned management consultant told me when asked the value of feedback. "We were right at the brink of catastrophe with a client that gives us $2 million worth of business.

"One of our firm's top people, a man, had insulted the number two person in the client's company, who was a woman.

"How did I rescue it?

"I went to the client and said, 'We have been working together a couple of years now. We have done a lot for you, and we are a member of your family. If your brother or your son makes a mistake or hurts your feelings, you don't automatically throw him out and replace him, do you? That's what you are doing with us. Why don't you sit down and tell us what the problem is? Like all good family members, we will correct it and see that it does not happen again.'"

This man was able to keep a very valuable customer because his feedback system let him know what his competitors were doing.

7. *Having the reputation of* wanting *to hear feedback can make money for you.*

Encouraging people to give you news, good or bad, requires that they trust you, that they think you will believe them and not scoff at their concerns. "Seventy percent of consumers do not complain because they don't know where to call, don't think it's worth the effort, or don't think companies will respond. . ." the *New York Times* reported March 26, 1988, on research done by the U.S. Office of Consumer Affairs.

By encouraging your customers to provide feedback, particularly complaints, you are showing concern, interest, *and the desire to satisfy* your customers. The very act of soliciting feedback is a positive signal to your clients. It also will make money for you by encouraging repeat business.

In a 1979 study conducted for the federal Office of Consumer Affairs, researchers queried people who had a problem with a product. This is what they found: Among those who had a problem but did not complain, 9.5 percent would rebuy. If the buyer complained but did not get satisfaction, 19.0 percent said they would rebuy. But of those who complained and got satisfaction, a whopping 54.3 percent said they would rebuy. The study also found that customers who have a good experience with your complaint-handling process tend to buy an accessory product.

In his book *Practical Handbook of Distribution/Customer Service*, Warren Blanding concludes that:

> "There is a measurable dollar value to the simple fact of getting customers to complain."

The Four Fatal Excuses That Undermine Feedback

Despite all this evidence of feedback's bottom-line value to a customer-driven organization, do you still choose to hide from feedback?

Here are some of the most common excuses managers use to evade feedback.

1. *"I don't ask because I'm afraid that the information will be too negative."*

The reality is that the information usually is much more positive than negative.

2. *"I feel inadequate about my ability to handle problem customers, so I avoid hearing complaints."*

To overcome this, I ask the customer-contact personnel in my seminars to role-play some of their real-life experiences with "problem" customers. First they act as representatives of their company. Then they switch roles and play the angry customer.

A "neutral" colleague observes and critiques the action, noting how well the employee responded to the problems and personality of the client. I encourage the employee playing the client to provide feedback to the customer service representative, such as "When you said _____, it made me feel _____."

This exercise boosts employees' confidence in dealing successfully with a problem customer. This exercise also forces the company to see its policies from the customer's point of view.

3. *"I do not solicit customer feedback because I feel it will create higher expectations than my company can fulfill."*

You can't give *all* customers *everything* they want. You do, however, need to determine the cost/service mix that will make you attractive to a large enough group of customers to generate a reasonable profit.

Do they want more strawberries on the buffet, or would they rather have kiwi fruit? Do they want their statements monthly or biweekly?

Get them to *prioritize their demands*, and focus on the top-ranked items. As a travel agent, you may be able to offer free ticket delivery, limo rides to the airport, and caviar—but the trip will cost $1,000. Without the frills, the price drops to $500. Which does your customer want: the lavish treatment or the lower price?

To get feedback in prioritized form (which I will discuss in more detail later), give the customer a forced-choice listing:

- Should the store open at eight A.M. or nine A.M.?
- Choose three of these five services that are important to you.
- Rank these ten services according to their importance to you.
- Which ten of these services would you scratch off this list of fifteen?

4. *"I don't get enough meaningful information to implement any worthwhile changes."*

You are spending extraordinary amounts of your resources (time, capital, people, credit, goodwill) on sophisticated accounting and financial systems, interior space design, promotion and market research, energy control, and inventory management. You correctly see these items as being essential to your efficiency. Why are you using an unsophisticated and haphazard feedback system when feedback is your lifeline to success?

If you feel that the feedback you've been getting has not been useful, ask yourself these questions:

- Do I ask enough questions?
- Do I ask the right questions?
- Do I communicate effectively about why I am asking the questions?
- Do I ask the right people?
- Do I know how to use the data I collect?
- Am I organized to respond to the information?
- Do I value and trust the information I receive?

If your answer to three or more of these questions is "no" or "I don't know," you are probably relying too much on what I call *incidental* information, or on *pass/fail information*. Such information often comes from countertop "tattletale cards," which ask yes/no questions that relate to a specific customer transaction or to the behavior of a particular employee.

Problems arise when you rely solely on incidental information because it tends to be *ad hoc* feedback that employees, in turn, tend to view as a witchhunt. While the information may help you identify inappropriate employee behavior so you can coach an employee to be more effective, it usually has little applicability beyond the single reported incident.

Pass/fail information is the kind that comes from countertop feedback cards like this one:

	Satisfactory	Fair	Poor
How would you describe the service you received?		X	
Please rate the appearance of our employees.			X
Are our business hours convenient?	X		

At the end of the month, you know that X number of customers think your service is only "fair." But *what* is it about your service that needs improvement? Is it too slow or too expensive?

Y number of customers are displeased with your employees' appearance. Is it their uniforms (wrong color, wrinkled, not functional)? Or is it their grooming (he needed a shave, her hair was unkempt, her skirt was too tight)?

Do the customers who find your business hours "satisfactory" appreciate the early-opening drive-through window, the late Thursday office hours, or the Saturday sessions? Let's say that you need to drop one of these services. Based on the survey data above, could you make an informed decision?

Those three pass/fail questions didn't give you enough information to make a decision, did they? You must go much deeper. First, ask questions that probe the underlying operational flaw that made the human transaction fail. Second, continually look for trends in the data you receive.

The customer questionnaire used by Sewell Village Cadillac of Dallas, Texas, fulfills both of these requirements. (See Appendix 2.) Its questions are specific: "Sewell Village has various methods of payment available. Was this discussed with you? Yes or No." "Was the Cashier polite?" "Was the Cashier helpful?" And there are fifty-five questions! (Note: Don't be afraid to ask for lots of information. If you make a questionnaire overly short and simple, the customer may decide that you are not really serious about it—and she will not take it seriously, either.)

With its form, Sewell Village is collecting what I call *operational information*. The data is specific enough to support adding or deleting systems, changing policies, or altering operations (including training or coaching of individuals) so that *the performance of the overall organization is dramatically enhanced*.

Don't let the four fatal excuses prevent you from revamping your feedback systems. The potential rewards will be worth it!

How I Get Feedback

We solicit feedback from every client after every speaking engagement, consultation, or training seminar. The most basic form of feedback I use comes immediately after I give a speech.

Naturally, there is applause from the audience—a heart-warming kind of feedback. Afterward, a certain number of people will come up to me and comment on the presentation or ask for more information. Their remarks and questions give me clues as to how clear my message was and how well I delivered it. I also ask the audience to fill out evaluation sheets right then and there, rating my performance as a speaker as well as the quality and relevance of the ideas I shared with them.

After the engagement is complete, I mail my clients an evaluation form. A sampling of the questions I ask:

- What were the strengths/weaknesses of the program presented for you by the Linda Goldzimer Consulting Group?
- What, if anything, about this program would you change? Why?
- What have you done operationally to carry forth the results of the program?
- How has the program affected performance and productivity?
- What did you value most from the total services you received from the Linda Goldzimer Consulting Group?
- What recommendations do you have as to how Linda Goldzimer Consulting Group can improve?

This first cluster of information concerns *the quality of the service* and the extent to which the service (in this case, my presentation, training session, and/or consultation and resource materials) benefited the client.

The next cluster of information covers *the relationship* the client had with my company: How did they like doing business with the Linda Goldzimer Consulting Group? I then review with my staff what went well and what didn't, comparing my impressions with the formal feedback.

Determine what you need to know from your customers and draft your own questions to obtain information that you can really *use*. I ask about my delivery; you may want to ask if the car you worked on last month is still running.

> **Ask operational questions and you'll get operational answers.**

Sources of Feedback: Whom Do You Talk To?

Whom do you talk to? Everybody. Why? Because the more threads of information you have, the more elaborate the tapestry you'll be able to weave from them. The image on this tapestry will be that of your company, as your customers see it. Here are nine suggested threads of your feedback fabric:

Feedback Source 1. Customer complaints
Source 2. Direct customer contact

Don't forget individual contact.
Conduct "exit interviews" with the customer.
Set up focus groups.
Arrange a captain's dinner.
Recognize the power of the home phone number.
Contact the end-user.
Track down the people whom you want as customers.
Talk to a variety of people within your customer's organization.

Source 3. Your own mail
Source 4. Formal customer survey
Source 5. Distributors and wholesalers
Source 6. Employee "special" sessions
Source 7. Staff meetings
Source 8. Your neighborhood
Source 9. Community involvement

Each thread is vital. As we go through the list, I'll show you how to get the most from each one.

Source 1: Customer Complaints

Complaints are the most common and direct form of customer feedback. No mystery here: The thing didn't work right and the buyer wants to know what you're going to do about it. *Now.*

Don't get shook up. Here are nine ways to deal with those angry customers:

1. *Respond immediately. How* the issue is handled is often more important than the solution itself. Give your customer a realistic, measurable time frame.

> *Wrong:* "We'll get back to you as soon as possible."
> *Right:* "We will call you at your office within two working days."

2. *Keep the customer informed of your progress.* If you haven't gotten the situation resolved within the two days mentioned above, *call anyway!* Angry customers prefer bad news to no news at all. It's the *expectation* that makes people anxious about waiting.

The Los Angeles County Sheriff's Department learned this through its feedback system, and began telling residents reporting less urgent matters that a car would be there in about forty minutes. After that, "there was no criticism of the response time," Sheriff Sherman Block said, "because they weren't standing at the front door waiting."

3. *Stress what you* can *do, not what you cannot do.* Try to give the angry customer choices. This makes him feel more in control, which dissipates his anger.

> *Wrong:* "I can't give you a cash refund."
> *Right:* "I am very happy to offer you another selection or issue you a gift certificate. Which would you prefer?"

4. *If possible, have your angry customer follow you into a*

private area where your conversation will not disturb everyone else. This shows that you care enough to provide personal attention and gives him a feeling that action is being taken.

5. *Don't challenge the customer.* Keep the conversation in the "I" or in neutral.

> *Wrong:* "You did not provide the information we needed."
>
> *Right:* "I failed to receive the necessary information."
> "The information we needed was not received."

6. *Don't try to win the argument.* Concentrate on finding solutions that both of you can live with.

The approach at the Boca Raton Hotel and Club, under Ted Kleisner's leadership, was that the customer is always right. Now, you, he, and I all know that the customer is not always right. How does Kleisner deal with that?

"You never try to justify the hotel's position in light of a guest complaint, showing how you are right and he is wrong. You just decide you are going to lose that one," he said.

In an extreme case, he added, "you may just say, 'Look, maybe you would be happier at the Fontainebleu.'"

7. *Allow the customer to vent his frustration and anger.* The angry customer is a speech in search of an audience. Only after he gives that speech will he be able to listen carefully enough to agree on a solution. Provide empathy: "I can appreciate how frustrating this must be for you."

8. *Find something to agree on.* It is difficult to argue with someone who is on the same side. Try a sentence that begins: "You're right. . . ."

9. *Always state the justification for your rules as a* benefit *to the customer.*

> *Wrong:* "I need to see some I.D."
>
> *Right:* "I need to verify everyone's signature, ma'am, to prevent the unauthorized use of your credit card."

Those are the nine essentials. I asked Kleisner how far beyond these essentials he would go to satisfy an unhappy client. "Have them back as our guests," he said. "That always works. If a person feels strongly enough that they did not get what we advertise as 'Quite Simply the Best,' we feel obligated to give them that experience and make certain it is memorable."

Mrs. Kaiserman (not her real name) got that "memorable experience" in a spectacular way. Mrs. Kaiserman enjoys an annual four-month stay at the Beach Club, Kleisner told me.

"Last year when she arrived, we had redecorated her suite and she did not like it." In her view, the new colors were wrong; the arrangement was uncomfortable. She liked it the way it was before.

"By that night," Kleisner told me, "we had all the old decor back."

Now, think about that for a minute. Within a few hours of the guest's complaint, her entire suite had been redecorated— chairs, sofas, lamps, bed, dressers, *wallpaper!*

No objections. No time wasted trying to talk her out of it.

Is Mrs. Kaiserman likely to keep coming back for her annual four-month stay? You bet! Is she likely to sing the hotel's praises to all her friends? Of course.

One Last Point: Do It with Style

When the situation is disagreeable or unpalatable, management and employees should follow the motto voiced by corporate strategist and professional speaker Pete Johnson: "When the disagreeable becomes the inevitable, do it with style."

An example: Mike and Connie were wholesale jewelry manufacturers from New York, visiting the Grand Brennen Hotel in Baden Baden, Germany, during the summer of 1985. According to Mike, "I went into the general manager's office to complain about our room. . . . I just didn't like it. And, do you know what he does? He gives me a glass of champagne. I couldn't believe it!"

Now, that's style.

Source 2: Direct Customer Contact

Another man with style, Jurg Reinshagen, managing direc-tor of the Palace Hotel in Lucerne, believes that the best feedback comes not from questionnaires, but from personal contact. He makes it a point to speak directly with every guest who stays three days or more. He recognizes that this is time-consuming, but he thinks it is the best way to collect their opinions of the hotel. He also talks to every guest as they check out.

• *Don't forget individual contact.*

Try this yourself. Answer an hour's worth of information-seeking calls to your 800 number every few weeks. Go to the stores where your shirts are sold and ask shoppers why they did—and especially why they didn't—buy your product.

• *Conduct exit interviews.*

Ted Kleisner's staff at the Boca Raton Hotel and Club in Florida conducted exit interviews with all group meeting plan-ners as they checked out of the hotel, while their thoughts were fresh, uncontaminated, and unblurred by subsequent events.

• *Set up focus groups.*

Kleisner also held focus groups made up of guests picked at random, as well as focus groups of outside meeting planners. A focus group is a gathering of customers specifically for the purpose of discussing your product or service. They are encour-aged to speak freely, and the sessions are sometimes videotaped for later review by all managers—a very useful practice. A statement coming "from the horse's mouth" will often have a stronger impact than the boss's pleas.

• *Arrange a captain's dinner.*

Hotel managers will frequently host cocktail parties for eight to ten guests, or host a "captain's dinner" a couple of days a week with randomly selected guests or representatives of major accounts. Relaxed dinnertime conversation will bring out new dimensions of the customers' experience. Try this with a group of your clients, and get them to talk about their relationship with your agency. The group dynamic may open your eyes to new perspectives and possibilities.

• *Recognize the power of the home phone number.*

"All our (outside) meeting planners get a letter from me after they book a meeting, saying . . . 'I want to help in every way to make your meeting a great success,'" Kleisner said. "And I give them my home phone number to call me if they can't reach me in the office."

Aghast, I asked him, "What percentage call you at home?"

"About one percent; next to nothing. But the percentage that write and say, 'I can't believe you did that' is almost ninety percent."

• *Contact the end-user.*

Go to the customer's plant and see how your machines are used. Ask the machine operators—the real customers—about maintenance problems, downtime, and ease of operation.

• *Track down the people whom you want as customers.*

"People will ask a lot of questions [of customers] when they get the order, but they won't ask the same questions when they lose [an order]," entrepreneur Ed Etess told me. "They are missing a valuable set of data . . . because of embarrassment or pride."

Etess suggests that if the salesman feels he must protect himself, he won't always give you the *true* reason why a sale fell through. His advice is to call the president of the firm that has just bought your competitor's product and say, "I'm disappointed that we didn't get the order. Please tell me how your decision was made." Then take that input to your salesman and talk it over with him, developing a strategy for the next order.

• *Talk to a variety of people within your customer's organization.*

Contact different people in different locations doing different things so you can get a well-rounded view of your firm's performance. Each person within your customer's organization perceives your company differently, depending on the nature of his or her job, personal biases, and personality.

For example, the secretary who is always breaking her nails

when trying to open the box that contains your typewriter ribbons may complain about your company incessantly. The trucker may not like your packaging because the boxes don't stack easily. The accountant may be unhappy because the third carbon copy of your invoice is too faint to read. Problems like these tend to build until the customer gets so annoyed that she snaps—and she'll never buy your product again.

Source 3: Your Own Mail

As many companies do, Ed Etess would send the customer a feedback form a few weeks after his equipment was delivered, asking:

- Do you like it?
- Was it delivered on time?
- Did it do what you expected?

And so on. "And," Etess said, "*I* would read the responses."
The president of the company would read what people wrote on postcards a month after they had begun using the product. "That was just another instance of closing the loop, of shortening the line between the end-user and myself," Etess said.

Source 4: The Formal Customer Survey

Since you can't talk to every customer yourself, look upon your formal customer survey as an extension of your outreach. Consider it your personal conversation with the customer.

"The more complex your organization, the more diverse product lines or service lines you have, the more you are in a national market, the more you have to rely on extensions of yourself, i.e., formal customer feedback surveys," says Paul Sanchez of Wyatt Company (whose advice on employee surveys appears in chapter 3).

A formal survey is designed to glean objective data: "Forty-one percent of subscribers like to have their newspaper delivered in a plastic bag every day—rain or shine." "Twenty-two percent of our guests prefer to be greeted by someone at the door of the hotel; the rest don't notice."

These are cold, hard facts. They are the acid test of your more subjective impressions.

Here are three important considerations when you design and implement your customer survey:

Ask Simple Questions

Ed Etess suggests the following questions. I have added a selection of responses to give you some ideas on how to adapt the questions to your needs.

- "What did you like about our product?" (a) Reliability (b) Choice of colors (c) Easy to maintain (d) Available nationwide (e) Other _____
- "What don't you like?" (a) Switch is hard to reach (b) Spare parts too scarce (c) Handle keeps breaking (d) Incompatible with existing systems (e) Other _____
- "What did you like about the competition's products?" (a) Less expensive (b) Lighter (c) More sales outlets (d) More models to select from (e) Other _____
- "What features are important to you?" (a) Portability (b) Durability (c) An 800 number to call if I have questions (d) Warranty (e) Other _____
- "Why did you buy from us before?" (a) I was desperate and needed the product quickly (b) Good reputation (c) Liked the salesperson (d) Catalogue purchases are convenient (e) Other _____
- "If our prices were higher, how would your choice differ?" (a) I would no longer buy this product (b) I would buy only twice a year (c) I would wonder how the quality had been improved (d) I would buy more often (e) Other _____

Give the customers a prioritized list as well: Would you like this or this? Which could you do without?

Design questions and offer choices of answers that will draw out the information that addresses your specific needs. As with your internal employee survey, set specific objectives and divide them into "chunks" of information. For example, service and communication were the subjects when the Walnut Creek, California, Police Department decided to conduct a citizen survey.

In his June 2, 1986, report on the survey, Sergeant David M. Johnson wrote down its six objectives. (I have adapted them slightly by plugging in the name of XYZ Company):

- To increase consumer awareness of XYZ Company's service/product
- To identify customer dissatisfaction with XYZ Company's services, products, practices, and employees
- To allow customer input on ways to improve our approach in providing service
- To increase employee awareness of our customers' expectations of and needs for XYZ Company's services/products
- To develop training to improve employee behavior when dealing with our customers
- To provide supervisors with a tool for evaluating subordinates' performance and behavior

Analyze the Results

After gathering the information, the Walnut Creek PD asked these questions:

- Has customer awareness of XYZ Company's services/products increased because of this survey?
- Have we identified areas in which our customers have been dissatisfied with our service/product? What are those areas?
- How can we apply these customer comments to improve our service/product?

- Are our own employees now more responsive to customer service needs and expectations?
- Have we developed appropriate training to improve employees' behavior toward customers?
- Are supervisors more aware of subordinates' behavior and performance, as well as customers' needs?
- Is the quality of the feedback adequate for us to evaluate the quality of our product or service? Are we asking the right questions in the right way?
- Is our evaluation of the feedback objective?

Implement the Results

You have a duty to do something with the results of the survey so that your employees, managers, and customers see that the survey was not just a waste of *their* time. But don't jump too quickly. When analyzing the data, try to distinguish between symptoms and diseases. Look for trends and underlying causes; don't lose focus by trying to treat every symptom (one common mistake that usually convinces managers that it's too difficult and time-consuming to deal with complaints). How you handle the issues raised depends on:

- The nature of the problem
- The degree of urgency involved
- Budgeting concerns
- Staff resources
- The existing cultural values of the organization—and how extensive your changes will be

The changes you make may range from asking one person to accomplish a concrete, immediate task to establishing a task force to look at overall policy. For example, one person may be able to implement a corporate change: by redesigning a form to make it clearer to the customers, or by drafting a preliminary corporate "Statement of Mission"—just as Thomas Jefferson wrote the Declaration of Independence alone.

For other situations, you may want to have greater companywide participation in bringing about changes. In that case, task forces, committees, work groups, and study groups would be appropriate. Although this obviously is slower, more costly, and may require more patience and leadership from you, it has the advantage of building broader "ownership" of the changes you want to make. People who have a stake in setting policy have an equal stake in seeing it successfully implemented.

In 1985, J. Kenneth Caresio, the city manager of Duarte, California, set out to eliminate the phrase "you can't fight City Hall" from residents' vocabularies by initiating what he calls a "pro-active, outreach approach to citizen input." He constructed a survey for citizens of Duarte, a city of 21,100 on the northeastern edge of the Los Angeles metro area. The survey is conducted in residents' homes, in the evening and on weekends, when they are most likely to be at home. Perhaps the best part of Duarte's survey process comes after a citizen completes the survey. If a specific concern or complaint is expressed, the surveyor *personally* follows up with the appropriate city department. This city employee then checks back with the resident to be sure the situation is corrected and finally *visits* the resident to verify that the problem has been addressed to the resident's satisfaction.

But implementation doesn't stop there. Monthly memos summarizing the survey's results are sent by the city manager to the city council, other department heads, the school superintendent, the commander of the local sheriff's office, the fire chief, and the head of the local chamber of commerce.

Strong follow-up, wide dissemination of the results, and changes in the way the agency operates—these are the keys to implementing the results of your survey. Having taken the time and effort to do the survey, it's to your advantage to go public with the results. Make sure that everyone—customers and employees alike—knows that you are taking action.

Source 5: Distributors and Wholesalers

Love gone wrong isn't the only thing you can hear via the grapevine that singer Marvin Gaye made famous. Also out on that grapevine are your distributors or wholesalers. When a deal has flopped, the distributor—who deals with the end-use customers as well as all of your competitors—often can give you a straightforward outsider's assessment. He also can tell you what the grapevine says about your competition.

It has been found that only 2 percent of consumers complain directly to the manufacturer. Most complaints go to retailers, wholesalers, and distributors. Since the manufacturer is far removed from the actual source of the complaint, it must tap as many sources as possible to obtain accurate feedback. This is how the network can become an extension of your sphere of influence.

Therefore, include your entire distribution chain—wholesalers, jobbers, distributors, and retailers—in your feedback circle.

Source 6: Employee "Special" Sessions

Your employees are the ones who implement your plans and frequently are closer to the customer than you are. Take advantage of their wisdom about your customers.

Try this exercise in your company: Convene groups of employees from different departments. Go around the room, asking each to respond to the question "What makes this company special?" Keep taking turns, going around and around the circle. The "loser" of the game is the person who finally cannot think of another reason why your company is special.

Having listed all the factors that make your firm special— what differentiates it in the marketplace and gives it its competitive edge—take that list and match it against what your customer survey shows that your customers want and need.

Are you special in ways that the customers don't care about?

Are the customers' current needs, future plans, and past problems being addressed? If you are being special in ways that the customers don't care about, it is a waste of time and money. And if you're not special at all, you're going to go out of business.

Source 7: Staff Meetings

John Singleton of Security Pacific Automation Company gathers employee feedback every day, and he *uses* the information to be sure things are running smoothly:

- He meets once a month with the vice-chairmen of all major customer groups and all of that person's key executives. They assess service levels, financial projects, and critical issues. At this meeting are all of his "direct reports and *their* direct reports," and they set the agenda. "We discuss whatever may be bothering them, positives and negatives." He encourages—and expects—total candor in these sessions.
- He hosts breakfast meetings every two months with half a dozen or so junior managers.
- He holds discussion groups with fifteen or twenty of the hourly workers. "And they know me well enough in this organization that they will talk about anything," he insists. "They do not hold back."

Singleton's employees can let loose because they know he keeps the source of the information gained in these sessions confidential. He'll tell a manager under him, "Several people think this is a problem." The manager may ask, "Who?" Singleton replies, "You know I'm not going to tell you who, but I want it fixed."

"I do not believe in filtered management," he said. Why? Because what filters up is subjective information that is only the *perception* of the upper level manager of what is going on below.

It sounds as though Singleton might step on a few toes in

middle management now and then. How does he overcome their feelings of having their authority threatened?

"I just do it," he said.

As he tells it, Singleton's top SPAC managers would say to him, "Why do you always know more about my organization than I do?" His reply: "Because I work harder at it. . . . If you want to know before I do, then I suggest you work harder, because I will not back off."

Singleton commented, "See, they were 'too busy' to meet with their people down below. They're working the 'filter' process."

Singleton's information comes from the heartbeat of the organization. He would hear that "people are going to quit. I would tell the [managers that] they had a morale problem. I would tell them they did not get the right percentage through on their raises and that they have twenty or thirty people who are very unhappy. They didn't know these things."

How did Singleton get the employees to talk to him without being intimidated?

"I would open up by saying, 'When I came up the ranks, here's what I found. Here's what I vowed I would never do. Here are the kinds of bosses I worked for. You've worked for some of those folks. No, none of us likes those kinds of bosses.

"'Help me change that. Help me make this the kind of place you want to work in, because if you don't trust me, then who are you going to trust?'"

Many managers for whom I consult become nervous at the idea of talking with younger workers, women, and minorities. They also may feel uncomfortable about leaving the security of the executive suite and revealing themselves to the employees.

"You have to work at being approachable," Singleton says. "And you're not born with that. I wasn't born with it. I had to work at it."

Singleton recognizes that his employees are his customers, so he goes out of his way to solicit feedback from them. If your employees know that you can't take bad news, they will soon stop giving it to you. And bad news is the news you need the most! With nothing but yes-men around you, you might as well be talking to yourself. Employee feedback prevents isolation—and the dangerous complacency it breeds.

Source 8: Your Neighborhood

Isolation can never kill a customer-driven company, because a customer-driven organization makes itself an integral part of the surrounding community. David Semadeni, general manager of the four-star Brazilian Court Hotel in Palm Beach, Florida, says that one of the best ways to learn about the reputation of your business is from your "neighbors."

Get to know the people in the community in which your business is located, and the community to which your business provides its service or product. Community input, David says, will "tell you a lot about how the guests are enjoying the hotel."

Source 9: Community Involvement

One man who has taken community input and turned it into a vehicle for success is Sheriff Sherman Block of Los Angeles County, California.

In 1986, 27,000 people applied for jobs to work for him.

With a fleet of sixty-three buses, he runs one of the biggest bus lines in the country.

He's responsible for medical services to approximately 17,500 people.

He operates eighteen helicopters plus two fixed-winged aircraft, 1,247 automobiles, and six thirty-foot boats.

His annual budget exceeds $450 million and he has 8,200 employees. More than 1,100 dedicated men and women volunteer their time and expertise to his organization.

Sitting across the luncheon table from Sheriff Block, I found it hard to reconcile reality with my expectations. After all, he is one of the leading law enforcement officials in the United States.

Based on my expectations and his stellar record, I had expected a cross between John Wayne and Clint Eastwood.

But there, munching on his salad, was the image of a caring, wise, strong, and approachable gentleman. To me, the sheriff looked more like my favorite uncle than a powerful public figure who is in his second four-year term, and who won 85 percent of the vote when he last stood for election, leaving his four opponents to split the leftovers.

"How do you know what your clients want and need from you?" I asked.

He replied, "One of the things we rely on is input from the community, and that comes from both the experience of our people working in that community, as well as . . . from a very large, very important volunteer component within the department.

"We have tried to focus on bringing in people who are representatives of the special components of the community, both to serve as interpreters—to help us communicate with these people in an official capacity—and to help us learn about culture, needs, and how to best approach their particular community to help them with their problems."

You can do this in your firm. Set up a standing customers' panel of community leaders to meet once a month and advise you. Call it a "customers' rights board." Get them involved with your company. Ask them about new product ideas. Let them give you feedback on potential logo designs. Have them review your job descriptions. Use this input when making your decisions. Besides the good information you receive, an important benefit of this panel is the goodwill it builds in the marketplace.

As they become intimately involved with developing your product or service, these people will have an enormous influence on the rest of your potential customers. Applying this principle to his volunteer program, Block says, "It is essential that people who have credibility and acceptance in the community be the ones to carry [our] message and try to serve as that link.

"We have tremendous impact, for example, in the Hispanic community dealing with gang violence. We went into the community and convinced the people that if they wanted to see violence reduced, if they wanted to see their children grow up instead of being shot down in wanton killings, if they wanted to be able to use their parks and walk their streets at all, then they had to assume a role in bringing this about."

> Get key customers involved in creating the service they want. And be sure that they see this as a bonus for them.

"We now have over eleven hundred volunteers," the sheriff said, "and believe it or not, every one has a specific assignment.

"Several times a year, I have a recognition dinner [honoring] about one hundred of the volunteers who contributed the most during the year. I ask each one to identify themselves, say a little bit about their personal life, and then tell me what they do for the department. Virtually without exception, they will stand up and say, 'I am in charge of . . .'

"Everybody is in charge of something, and they really have taken a proprietary interest."

> Once the customer takes a proprietary interest in your business, she starts to look out for your success.

"Sometimes our actual accomplishments are less important than our perceived accomplishments. Statistically, the crime rate may not go down one iota. But if we undertake a series of programs that give high visibility and a sense of well-being, [causing] the people [to] *feel* more secure—even though the crime rate is not going down—then we have . . . affected the quality of life of these people; we have accomplished a great deal."

> The clients' *perception* of your product's bene-
> fit is what determines client satisfaction. Your
> feedback network not only tells you what your
> clients are thinking; it helps you to influence
> what they think.

Credibility Grows from Your Feedback Network

You know by now that trust is necessary to get the initial feedback. The amazing thing is that once you've established that trust, your willingness to listen will inspire customer confidence in your organization. This creates a synergism that magnifies the effects of your efforts.

Sheriff Block has established a strong customer relationship with the Baptist Ministers Conference, a group of about 400 black ministers in Los Angeles County. He did it by making them a promise, and standing by it.

"The first time I appeared before this group, they were going to determine whether or not they should endorse me politically, which they don't normally do," Block recalled.

"They set up a committee to interview me, and the question was, 'Anytime there's a serious problem in the community, will we have access to your office to discuss it with you?'

" 'No,' I said.

" 'What do you mean, "No"?' they said.

"I told them, 'I have no interest in establishing a relationship in which a dialogue [occurs] only when we have a problem. What I'm interested in is establishing a relationship and a dialogue so that we can prevent these problems from occurring in the first place.'

"I said, 'If you feel a need to see me, of course I would appreciate your calling and making an appointment to set up a time. But if it's something that has to be addressed more urgently, then come on by. I may not see you immediately; you may be waiting in my outer office for two hours or more. *But I will see you.*'"

About a week later, his secretary buzzed him and said that a minister was waiting in the office to see him. "I said, 'I'll get to him as soon as I can, but please tell him it may be thirty to forty-five minutes before I can get some free time.'

"So he waited, and I finally got out, greeted him, and said, 'Now, what can I do for you?'

"He said, 'You already did it. You made a statement at our meeting that if we ever had a need to see you, to come on down. And you did exactly what you said you were going to do. I'm going to tell the rest of the group that you were not just talking.'"

> **Don't try to build a bridge after the creek has risen: Create a feedback relationship designed to prevent problems from occurring in the first place.**

"This group has helped us become the only county in California that received a two-thirds vote to pass a jail bond issue. "We're now in the process of trying to site a new jail. And the ministers are speaking from the pulpit in support of our efforts."

> **As you build your feedback systems with your customers, the payoff is *real*.**

5

Interviewing and Selecting
Stellar Staff

"Hire a Who, not a What."
—LINDA SILVERMAN GOLDZIMER

American Airlines Flight 155 had left JFK at 6:45 P.M. on its way to Lindberg Field in San Diego, California. The dinnertime debris had been collected, the cocktail cups were drained, the movie had become a memory. It was the time during every long flight when passengers begin to ask themselves, "Are we there yet?"

I looked up wearily and saw flight attendant Joni Strong walking slowly down the aisle with a huge puppet wrapped around her waist and shoulders. The puppet resembled a chimpanzee, with big "ET" eyes and long, silky light brown hair, its arms and legs clasping Joni tightly.

Wearing a San Diego Padres baseball cap and a T-shirt with "Buffy 5" on the back, the puppet "walked" up and down the aisle talking to everyone, with Joni providing the voice. The passengers responded enthusiastically. They laughed, joked, and talked with Buffy, patting his head.

Joni told me that she had been working with Buffy for about three years. She does it because she gets such a positive reaction from the passengers. According to Joni, when passengers are sitting and not doing much, Buffy cuts through the barriers and allows them to begin conversations with one another. The surprise and smiles make the trip more enjoyable for everyone. Joni Strong has a strong personal involvement and interest in her customers.

Why? My guess is that it's because she's made that way. In your business, employees can improve or destroy your firm's relationship with your customers. Are your employees like Joni? Or do they have more in common with the one-woman wrecking crew described below?

I was tired, it was late, and the temperature in the restaurant where I was dining at a hotel in Glendale, California, that July evening was just above freezing. I mentioned to my waitress that the air conditioning was much too cold, and asked if she might be able to raise the temperature of the room so that the other guests and I would not have to hear our teeth chattering. Her responses, in rapid succession: "I have no control over the temperature." "I can't get you a sweater." "You are welcome to move to another table."

I did move to a different table, not so much to get away from the cold draft (which was impossible), but to get away from *her*. When I registered the same complaint with my new waitress, her unhesitating response was, "I will call the front desk to see if they can make the room warmer."

When she returned from the bar with the drink I had ordered, she carried a jacket borrowed from the front desk clerk and said she had inspected the jacket to be certain that it was clean. (P.S.: The air conditioning was indeed adjustable, and everyone in the dining room was eventually more comfortable.)

Instead of "I can't," her reply to my request for assistance was "I will." I had dealt with two waitresses in the same dining room, but their attitudes were 180 degrees apart.

Why do some of your employees know the right response to a situation, while others do not?

The answer ends with how you train them and how you manage them.

It begins with the simple fact that a person behaves the way he does because of his inner qualities, values, attitudes, and personality. You can change behavior, but you can't change personalities.

> **Hire the kind of person who can build strong customer relationships.**

One of the most expensive decisions you make is the hiring of a new employee. Advertising, moving expenses, plane tickets for interviewees—the cost can be staggering, especially for small businesses. Turnover in personnel can stall your initiatives, and the hidden cost of orientation, retraining, supervision, and waiting for them to know enough about the job so that they do more good than harm is unquantifiable.

"Just think how expensive it is when you make a mistake: severance pay, distress suits, worker's compensation, unemployment insurance," said Paul Whisenand, a noted personnel consultant. "The only thing that is more difficult than getting rid of a bad employee is finding a good employee." While you may have been schooled in delegation, control, planning, investing, and communicating, few managers are instructed in how to select their personnel.

Using techniques I have developed in my work as a high-level executive and staff development trainer, along with concepts gleaned from other successful executives, I will show you a five-step formula for building a team that will help you create your customer-driven company. First, get some paper and a pen or pencil. As we go through the hiring process, jot down some of the ways that these ideas apply to your agency. By the end of the chapter you'll know:

- What steps to take in hiring not only a good person, but the *right* person

- How to determine what the person in that job really does, and the importance of making that determination
- How to construct ads and job descriptions that will show your applicants—and new employees—their connection to the customer
- How to predetermine your new employees' success on the job
- How to build a recruitment process that will work for you as never before
- Ways to set up screening and selection procedures that yield consistently good results
- How to add up all these selection factors and make a hiring decision

Take Control of Hiring

First, *you must take control of the selection process yourself.* Otherwise, it will be performed by other people in your division who know much less about whom you need, or by some centralized personnel function. When you are not intimately involved, all the damage from poor selection will be magnified.

From my work with companies and local governments all over the nation, I've concluded that most organizations hire primarily on the strength of the resume. They concentrate almost exclusively on a candidate's education, technical competence, years of experience, and (maybe) references.

I tell my clients that they must go beyond these points if they want to become customer-driven.

If you are like most managers, you concentrate on these areas because you perceive them as "safe." Technical skills, training, and experience are relatively easy to measure. Can she use the tools and machinery necessary? Has he mastered the technology of the job? Does she have the required information at her command?

This method is conservative and generally is viewed as being cost-effective. It also does not work very well.

In my experience, managers continue to follow this procedure because they know of no alternative methods and because they worry about violating equal employment opportunity laws, affirmative action requirements, and the applicant's right to privacy.

These are valid concerns, but being overly cautious means that lawyers and fear of potential litigation end up running your company instead of you.

I can alleviate this fear by helping you understand the restrictions imposed by the law. You can then apply that understanding, along with your own reasonable and appropriate judgment and the advice of qualified professionals.

A Word of Caution

Your customers come in all races, creeds, and colors—and so should your employees. That is the law, both federal and in the marketplace. To abide by equal employment opportunity laws, you must seek the information you need in a careful, appropriate manner.

As long as the information will provide an accurate indication of successful performance on the job, your intelligent, well-planned interview and selection process remains within the law. The process can be flexible and creative enough to help you staff your organization with the talent you need to become customer-driven.

In Appendix 3 are the State of California Pre-Employment Inquiry Guidelines. They give examples of questions that generally are considered fair and relevant. This information, however, is no substitute for the advice of your lawyers. Don't throw out the good advice of a qualified attorney. But you must find your own way in this thicket of employment practices. *I am offering a process that you can use or not use. You are responsible for seeing that it is used in a lawful manner.* With that said, let's move on to the five steps of building a team that will help you compete and win in today's customer-driven market.

Step 1: Analyze the Job

A major reason why companies mismatch employees with positions is that managers have no idea what their staff really does. Most jobs are described in terms of the *processes* to be performed. We rarely speak about *what the person in that job is supposed to accomplish*. Ask these questions about the job:

- What impact does this person have on my customer?
- What is the result of her labors?
- Why does this person come to work in the morning?

Comedian George Carlin does a wonderful routine about people's emotional attachment to their "stuff." Carlin describes how we carry our stuff around with us from house to house, from job to job, into hotel rooms, and into other people's homes. Our stuff makes us feel at home, so that we feel comfortable and safe. It becomes part of our identity.

In the workplace, people tend to define their jobs in terms of the "stuff" the job produces—the tangible, measurable part of the job. Stuff is what fills your in-basket. It rarely has to do with the impact of the work we do. (I like to note that one of Webster's definitions of stuff is "writing, discourse, or ideas of little value." It lists "trash" as a synonym!)

Your employees want to do a good job. They work all day and leave the office in the evening tired, often with a briefcase full of stuff to read at home. But what have they done to promote or solidify the relationship between your company and your customer? Are they too attached to the routine to be flexible?

Examine the results, not the stuff, you want the employee to produce.

Employees often emphasize the stuff instead of the result of their work because the people who hire them usually concentrate on the stuff. But that's in past. *You're* in charge of hiring now.

"OK, Linda," you say. "I have this vacancy to fill. How do I determine what characteristics a candidate needs to succeed in this job?" You asked the right question that time!

First, Ask the Customer

Paul Whisenand comes across as a good-natured, positive individual with a flair for practical jokes. He is frequently quoted as saying that people want to have fun at work, and he told me he wishes that business schools would take down the imaginary signs over their doors that declare, "Those Who Enter Here May Never Smile Again."

A former police officer with a doctorate in public administration, Paul is president of PMW Associates in San Clemente, California. His firm specializes in personnel selection and human resource development for both public and private sector clients.

"When doing your job analysis, ask your customers what they want to experience when they walk in your front door, look across the counter, or look across the desk," Paul said.

Ask them:

- What kind of person do you want to see when the paramedics arrive?
- How do you want the serviceman to greet you?
- When you walk in to pay your bill, what do you want to experience from across the counter?
- When you place an order, what do you expect from the salesperson?

Agreeing with this assertion, David Semadeni, general manager of the Brazilian Court Hotel in Palm Beach, Florida, told me, "I always examine my first impression [of job applicants], because that is how the customer will see them. Hotel guests rarely have an opportunity to develop a long-term relationship with our staff. So first impressions are not only lasting, they are critical to the overall impact we have on our guests."

Jacques Rey, the proprietaire-directeur of the five-star Crans Ambassador Hotel in Crans-Montana, Switzerland, displays the kind of sensitivity in selection that earned the resort its five stars. "Certain positions must establish trust and inspire confidence on the part of the guest," he told me while sitting in the bar of his hotel. "My main barman was a good-looking Austrian, a nice person, but he was not selling enough drinks.

"I thought a younger man at the bar might be good because he would be more aggressive at sales."

But the younger man was smaller, and "because of his presence and stature, did not inspire the kind of confidence that was needed for our more wealthy, free-spending guests to order Dom Perignon champagne," Rey said. "We stayed with the original barman because of his more impressive presence."

Back in the U.S.A., Yvonne Oberle, manager of the Del Mar branch of Great American Savings and Loan, knows that she has well-informed, sophisticated customers. She seeks to hire knowledgeable people who won't be overwhelmed by a casual reference to convertible debentures.

"You start with the client," Paul Whisenand said. "From there, you build a profile that you can cast into a job description."

The Teamwork Factor

"How would you hire, say, an engineer?" I asked Whisenand. "Someone who might never see the external customer?"

He replied, "I would say to the people within the organization, 'We're going to hire a new engineer. He's going to work with the equipment maintenance director. What kind of *person* do we need?'

"In relation to the people he will be working with, do we need a competitor or a compromiser? Do we need a problem-solver? Do we need a helpmate or a loner?" Paul asks.

"The *last* thing you ask is, 'Hey, do you know how to handle an electronic calculator and are you in fact an engineer?' Because those are by far the easiest things to come by. All the rest precedes that."

How well will the potential employee fill the *role* that the job requires? Can he complement the other people in the organization? Is she capable of getting her work done—with cooperation and mutual respect? Does he shower often enough? (A more common problem than you might think!) Has she ever resigned at lunchtime on her third day at a new job?

"If you hire a person based on his Ph.D. in civil engineering," Paul said, "but he refuses to cooperate with the equipment maintenance director, and he irritates all the people he works with, you're going to have a person who is *potentially* very, very productive but who isn't capable of getting any work out or helping to get anybody else's work out."

When building your customer-driven team, play to your strengths by hiring to your weaknesses.

I find that, when I meet people who have excelled at their work, it is rarely because of their technical competence alone. They have found the right way to deal with people. Not everyone has that ability.

The short tenure of medical partnerships, for example, is legendary. Partnership breakups match the current 50 percent divorce rate in marriages. The differences that lead to dissolutions:

- One is there twelve hours a day, the other six.
- One is gruff, one soothing with patients.
- One pulls in new business, the other complains about the workload.
- When it comes to billing and collections, one is tough, the other is forgiving.

- One will hire only experienced office staffers, the other wants trainees because they'll work cheaper.
- One has no interest in hospital politics, the other plays the game of power relationships—to win.

Rarely do professional associations dissolve because the partners practice the art and science of medicine differently. Yet type of training, years of experience, number of papers published, hospital affiliations, and other "stuff" are often the only factors considered in forming such a partnership. The *real* issues, such as those listed above, are hardly considered and seldom discussed beforehand. They certainly never appear in the job description or recruitment announcement when a partnership is being formed.

Tell your employees what they *really* need to do to be successful at work.

My Hiring Values

The list of qualities I look for in new employees starts with *loyalty* to the company—and, frankly, to me (after all, in my business, I am the product). I want my employees to feel like *stakeholders* in our enterprise and its success.

I can't tolerate a nine-to-fiver. I expect a tremendous amount of commitment to the job, to the quality of the work, and to our customers. While asking for a strong commitment, I am very supportive. I understand and acknowledge the pressures that outside problems can create. I know that some personal appointments (lawyer, doctor, or real estate agent) will occur during business hours, and I am flexible.

But I also expect that when a special project has to be turned out, that person will be there. If she has to bring in her own computer for extra printing capacity, she does it. If her son is too sick to go to school, if her day care center is flooded, she brings him into the office and gets the work out while he sleeps in the next room. I look for that positive, "can-do" attitude.

Then I look for *initiative,* paired with *creativity.* I want to hear creative, resourceful solutions to problems. I want to see some risk-taking. If you then make a mistake, it's because you were performing as a mature professional, willing to take on responsibility, willing to exercise judgment, willing to be held accountable. When you *do* make a mistake, admit it. Some things just work out better than others. I reward the decision as well as the outcome.

The anchor for my list is *honesty. Total honesty.* A cover-up or an omission is as bad as a lie, in my eyes.

That is my list. And I truly do base my hiring decisions more on these personality factors than on technical ability—which almost always can be easily learned by the type of person I just described.

"Well, Linda, Be on Time!"

Communicate your *personal* values to your staff. When I was one of the 6,700 employees in a major organization, I reported directly to the assistant chief executive. Shortly after I was promoted to head a major line department with 225 employees, a very diverse revenue base, an extremely varied clientele, and a $52-million budget, I walked into my boss's office and asked, "In your opinion, what is the most important thing I can do to succeed in this job?"

I, of course, expected a replay of a traditional, process-oriented job description.

He looked me in the eye and said, "Well, Linda, be on time!"

My boss expected me to perform the functions of my job well, so he didn't mention that. He was telling me his underlying, personal value—a personal preference that had little to do specifically with the official job but that ultimately would increase substantially my success in his eyes. He is *always* on time, and it bugs the heck out of him when other people are not.

We all know how these "little" unspoken irritants build up over time. You may never even think of analyzing your own feelings about these factors. But these unarticulated values play a large role in the success of your employees. Make a list now of the attitudes and attributes you want to see in the person you will hire to fill the upcoming vacancy. Add to this list by taking attributes of your best employees and drawing a "sketch" of the ideal employee for that job. Use "Pam's intelligence," "Glenn's confidence," "Julie's work habits," and so on. Keep technical competence off the list! You're examining the individual here, not the process of the job. Keep this list handy as you study the next steps.

Step 2: Write a Job Description That Does the Job

A job description is a document that identifies what your employee is expected to do. "Be on time" should be in there if that's what you want.

Whether or not it's a customer contact job, the official description should declare very precisely the job's connection to the customer.

Tell the computer analyst that his efforts should help get products to the customer faster. Notify the gardener that he's trimming the lawn so the company's visitors will see the right image.

Say: "This job requires a caring, committed individual who takes pride in his/her . . ."

Say: "The customer benefits from your work by receiving his/her bill on the tenth of every month, with little variation."

Of course, you should also list the desired knowledge and skills, just as you do today. But *always* write your job descriptions to ensure that they go beyond technical and functional skills (the what) and delineate the personal traits you seek (the who). (Your job description should say, "We want a person who . . ." instead of "This position requires . . ." You'll never hire a position; all your applicants are people.) Otherwise, you might well end up with an employee who is more adequate than excellent.

Step 3: Make Recruitment Work for You

Where do the best applicants come from? From your "I'M FIRST" recruitment process, naturally.

"To get *a* good idea, you ought to have *a lot* of ideas," as Paul Whisenand of PMW Associates says.

Take your time with recruitment. Cast a very wide net and carefully sift through what you catch in it.

The Job Announcement That's Worth Its Cost

In your advertisements, talk about the job in human terms. Recruitment bulletins never say, "It is fun to work for this city," or for this company, Whisenand remarked. Job announcements rarely declare, "Here is a set of mission statements." "Here is a description of our organizational culture." "Here are five key values of the people who work here."

What they do say, Whisenand joked, is: "Salary is _____. Fringe benefits are _____. You're expected to type, walk straight, and . . ." This type of ad gives the applicant no idea what it's like to work with you. *"Let the potential job applicant know that this is a living organization,"* Paul said.

Here are two wildly different job recruitment ads from the Sunday *Los Angeles Times* (January 3, 1988):

SOFTWARE CONFIGURATION SENIOR ANALYST. Will gather and extract engineering accounting data to assist in the preparation of specifications, baseline technical descriptions, and configuration indices. Responsibilities include maintenance of current configuration control systems, status accounting statistics and assistance in the Configuration Control Board, and chairing Engineering Change Proposal activity. Will also plan subordinate functions associated with program contractural requirements. This position requires good writing ability and three-to-five years of experience in configuration and/or software configuration management activities which have complied to DOD and MIL-SPEC Standards. B.S. or B.A. in Business, Computer Science, or Engineering.

I wonder if "this position" ever gets a lunch break. If your job announcements and recruitment ads resemble this, throw them out and start over. For contrast, read this ad (same day, same page):

The continued advancement [of what this firm manufactures] requires the concerted efforts of intelligent and innovative people. People with determination and creativity. People like you. We are currently offering the following opportunities to put your abilities to the test.

Now, this is much more effective. "We need intelligent, determined, creative people around here," it says. "We will put you to the test."

This firm "offers an attractive salary, comprehensive benefits, and a professional, growth-oriented work environment." Work environment! The guy described in that first ad had no work environment. They wanted him to "chair Engineering Change Proposal activity." Anybody who recruits for someone to "chair activity" has left people out of the picture.

> Target your recruitment bulletins very specifically and describe the job in human terms.

Here is an excellent job announcement that was posted at the *Los Angeles Times* for a writer in its bureau in Nairobi, Kenya. It was written by Foreign Editor Alvin Shuster, and it decribes the job in human terms:

This is a fascinating, wide-ranging, exhausting assignment and often involves certain difficulties: Sometimes you can't get from there to here, or from there to there, or even from here to here, but, somehow, one does it anyway. Happily, lots of great scenery, lions, zebra, and game parks, but sadly, lots of coups and famine, and worse.

In those two sentences, Shuster crystallized the real-life experience of working in Africa. Write a brief announcement like this one for the next vacancy you have. Be honest and inventive, decribing the real-life environment the person will work in. It may not be the African bush, but your company does offer challenges to prospective applicants. Describe them.

Beat the Bushes

How do you draw herds of applicants to your door? Bring out your tracking gear and hunt for them.

"The top three finalists should be those that you went out and appealed to," Paul Whisenand said. "Rarely do we see an employer going out and taking a strong, pro-active posture and seeking out the best."

The Villa d'Este, a 180-room, 200-employee, world-class, five-star hotel in Lake Como, Italy, does reach out. Manager Mario Arrigo was frank in admitting to me that one of his key selection processes is to *seek out the best people* in the industry regardless of where they work, *then hire them* into Villa d'Este. His department heads work at other major hotels during the winter season, such as St. Moritz, and pick the best people from these and other places.

"The best [candidate] is typically on the sidelines," Whisenand said, "thinking, 'You know, I don't have to get into this game unless I want to.'"

To find these people, "blanket potential candidates with mass mailings directly to organizations and professional trade journals," he added. Get on the telephone to call everyone you know who can recommend successful applicants to you.

Agencies and Referrals

Joyce Ross is a partner in Ross/Lewis & Associates. She specializes in personnel assessment and is an expert in the personnel field. A former professor at San Diego State University, she is a walking bibliography on the latest concepts of successful selection.

"If you're using employment agencies or executive recruiting firms," Ross said, "spend enough time with the recruiters so that they understand your firm's philosophy and are sensitive to the special type of person you want to hire."

About recruiting, she said, "Internal sources such as employee referrals and walk-ins are the most powerful and most effective ways to get good employees.

"You have an advantage with referrals from people who work in your organization because they already know the organization. These applicants have already heard from their friends about what's good and what's bad. So you don't have to worry about the disillusionment that sometimes comes in the first couple of weeks or months on the job."

Go to the trade shows and meet people. Ask your employees whom they've admired at other companies that might be your kind of person. Call up the sharp executive you met at the monthly chamber of commerce luncheon; he may be ready to make a move. Take the time to search for talent.

Step 4: Insiders' Tips on Interviewing

Now we're ready to script the interview. What did you ask the last job applicant whom you interviewed? Did you ask about more "what" than "who"?

- "Where did you get your engineering degree?"
- "How many years have you been working as a mechanic?
- "Are you user-friendly with a personal computer?"
- "Do you understand computer-assisted manufacturing?"

Don't be surprised if you answered, "yes." Most people do. However, you want a more in-depth, *personal* examination of the individual.

"It is the people skills that are rarely analyzed and almost always make for ultimate success or failure. This is true even where specific technical competencies are vital, like medicine, law, and engineering," said Phil Blair and Mel Katz, executive officers of San Diego's eight Manpower Services offices, one of the most successful Manpower franchises and part of the network of 1,300 Manpower offices in thirty-two countries.

List the characteristics and skills that you feel are necessary for success. Now rank them, putting the most important ones at the top of the list. Ask questions that help you see how well the prospective employee will mesh with your company's value system.

- Use a case study to find out how she rates following the rules versus complying with the customer's wishes.
- Ask what motivates her. Is it acceptance, achievement, money, or power?
- Ask about her perception of her greatest strength or weakness.
- Ask, "Are you and your best friend alike or different? What do you admire most about your best friend?"

The questions should be a combination of approaches.

Direct questions: "Was there any big blow-up at your last job that made you quit? Or was your parting amiable?"

Leading questions: "What in your past work or life experience is most pertinent to the position we're talking about? What did you learn from that experience?"

Open-ended questions: "What do you want to tell us that we haven't given you an opportunity to say? What are *your* questions?"

Situational questions: "You are the supervisor of three clerk/ typists. One is habitually late. Although she is compatible, does a good job, and *is very well liked by your clientele,* you feel strongly about tardiness. It is a small office. How would you handle it?" Design your questions to solicit the information you really want to know. I remarked to Joyce Ross that the universal reply to the question "Do you like to help people?" is, "Yes, yes, yes." She noted that the real questions to ask applicants for public contact positions are along the lines of "How do you react when you have to deal with angry, miserable, frustrating, insolent, irate people?

"Ask, for example, 'If a customer comes to you and holds you responsible for something you haven't done, how do you feel?'" Joyce said.

"If the applicant says, 'I get really upset and stew about it later,' that person probably will not be able to handle that job and the stress that comes with it."

> Ask questions designed to uncover what you want to know about the *person* you are interviewing, as well as to assess how he or she will fit into the actual environment of the workplace.

Formula for Successful Selection

"An excellent staff is not created by happenstance or sheer intuition," said Sharon Canter, a corporate spokeswoman for the president of Manpower Temporary Services in the company's headquarters in Milwaukee, Wisconsin. Manpower had created a profile of the behavioral style that is necessary to be successful as a Manpower Service representative. Proven over time, this profile earns the title of "validated." It is seen as an accurate predictor of success on the job, with no disproportionate impact on any protected class of people.

The list of winning qualities:

1. Empathy and patience
2. Willingness to follow through
3. Poise and confidence
4. Decisiveness and independent judgment
5. Calm, controlled style
6. Energy and alertness

This list works. Manpower strives to draw out these customer service skills by asking open-ended questions such as:

- What do you do to build lasting rapport with people you meet?
- What work situations have required special patience and tact with people?
- What are some problems you have faced when dealing with people?
- How have you handled these problems?

In an industry where people are the only product, Manpower employs this carefully targeted interview process. It seems to be succeeding: When Mel Katz and Phil Blair bought the San Diego offices in 1977, the firm was grossing about $350,000 a year. This year, the figure is $27 million.

Face to Face

The interview should be fun for everyone involved. Yes— fun. Put the candidate at ease, establish rapport, introduce yourself and others by name and title. If there is more than one interviewer present, having nameplates on all the interviewers' desks helps the applicant. Be sure to smile, relax, and maintain eye contact. Also remember: The interviewee is there to do the talking. You are there to listen.

In addition, observe the applicant's nonverbal communications. Many of these are obvious: neat appearance, eye contact, upright posture. But there are subtler signs that many psychologists have written about—and all of these can reveal the personality of the person you are evaluating. Gestures and speech habits add nuances to the conversation.

With all this in mind, recognize that *both the applicant and the employer are trying to determine whether this is a good match*.

Allow for Self-Selection

Yes, the applicant is making an important decision, too. *He must decide whether he can (and wants to) do the job*. If the job description, job announcement, recruitment process, and interview itself are conducted as I describe, most unsuitable candidates will have eliminated themselves by this stage because they recognize that their chances for success are limited. The finalists should be invited to tour your shop, to meet and talk with as many people as possible—particularly current employees holding similar jobs, and employees who might be working for the applicant.

Let him see how close together people sit, hear the office banter, touch the desk he might be using, use the telephone system—and decide for himself whether he fits in. This will either turn him off or turn him on. If his reaction is negative, you're much better off finding out before he is hired.

I know of a very competent man who lasted only five months at a job where he could handle all of the "stuff" impeccably. His downfall was the telephone. About twenty phone calls a day were required to coordinate his office's efforts with those of two other remote offices. But he was uncomfortable using the telephone. He had no hearing problem, just an uneasiness that prohibited him from communicating effectively over the phone. Had he realized beforehand how much telephone time was involved, he might never have taken the job. (You can be sure that this firm now asks *all* applicants for that job if they have any trace of "phonophobia.")

Letting applicants tour the workplace pays off for June Hendershot, personnel director for Great American Savings & Loan. "For example, at the teller line, we want people capable of and comfortable with providing warm greetings while still being efficient and being able to handle the cash. . . . I talk about this specifically," she said.

"I ask [candidates if they] get nervous if people are waiting in line. . . . Then I ask them to go to the branches and talk to the tellers, the new accounts people—the people who work for us now. The applicant will then come back if he likes what he hears."

You save a lot of money by recognizing that some people will disqualify themselves if you give them the opportunity.

Exposing the job candidate to the workplace is a very efficient tool for finding the right employee, because he knows himself better than you ever will.

How to Use Work Samples

A tool called *work samples,* or assessment centers, can help you create situations that are representative of the work the applicant would have to do. Ask her to perform in a hypothetical situation, while you observe. "It's much closer to what they actually do on the job than asking them a question," Joyce Ross told me.

"I find [work samples] to be one of the most powerful ways to begin to get real clarity on whether this person is really the individual we want."

"In one case," said John Singleton of Security Pacific Automation Company, Inc., "we took a systems programmer down to the computer center and said, 'The system went down. Can you get it back up?' And he did so. So in that instance, we took him into a real-life situation. We said, 'If we're going to hire you, this is what you will do, so tell us what you'll do.' That shocked him. It was very unusual pressure, but I thought it was fine."

Newspapers for years have given job applicants a paid "tryout." A copy editor will work for a week on the copy desk of his prospective employer, meeting his potential coworkers, employees, and bosses in the workplace. The interviewee participates in daily meetings, edits deadline stories for publication, and goes to dinner with the rest of the crew. It's essentially a five-day job interview.

Character insights arise from the informal moments that occur during a work week. Coworkers are also part of the process; their input helps in assessing how well an applicant will mesh with the rest of the team.

Peer Selection and Group Interviewing

Compared to other development firms, Fieldstone Company, the eighth-largest home builder in southern California, has a very low personnel turnover rate. The firm built and sold $175 million worth of homes in 1986. In 1987, the figure was $200 million. Tall, well groomed, and well tailored, CEO Keith Johnson reflects his success. His tightly scheduled calendar and active alarm wristwatch gave me the impression that he makes optimal use of his time.

To get maximum effectiveness in hiring, he involves a wide variety of employees in the interview process, and he knows what "people characteristics" he wants.

"A Fieldstone person is someone who is willing to work hard, who cares about the outcome of their efforts, who cares that they are making a positive contribution, who is congenial with fellow workers, and [who] has a very high level of integrity. We look for people with those same values."

The top two candidates for a job—survivors of an initial screening by their potential supervisor—"will be interviewed by virtually everyone with whom they will work—subordinates, superiors, peers," Johnson said.

People using this approach feel that employees who participate in the hiring process "achieve a degree of ownership in the decision and are somewhat more committed to it," he told me.

> **Create wide ownership of the success of the new employee by expanding the circle of interviewers.**

Also, with so many people interviewing the applicants, you get what I like to call a 360-degree view of the person.

The interviewers hold a brainstorming session to discuss the two finalists. During this session, one person typically will have a question about the applicant and another employee will say, "Oh, yeah, I know about that."

Topics discussed:

- How honest is the person?
- How does the person react when a problem arises?
- How well will she supervise people?
- How will he fit in with current employees?

Another dimension (the most important one) is "their degree of commitment to the value of what they contribute," Johnson said.

If Fieldstone is interviewing, say, a potential field superintendent, and the applicant lists cost control, scheduling, and estimating as things that are important to him on a job, but he never brings up the quality of the product, "that would tell us a lot about him," Johnson said.

"If we talked to a guy who took a great deal of pride in having a family move into the home *he* built, and that it was the excitement that *they* get out of *their new home* that was important to him . . . he's the kind of guy we're looking for. . . .

"Nothing is better than the genuine sense of caring that's inside the person . . . caring about the quality of the product we are giving to our customer."

Fieldstone's peer selection system is similar to that employed by Sheriff Sherman Block of Los Angeles County. "I

believe that the best people to select deputies are not lieuten-
ants and not captains, but other deputies who are out there
doing the job," Block told me. "They can look at these potential
new deputies in the context of: 'Is this the kind of person I may
want to work with as a partner some day?' And 'Does this person
fit into the organization as I know the organization to be?' "

Answering that last question is the entire object of my five-
step interview process.

So let's say that . . .

- You have formulated a variety of questions to identify the
  characteristics that will guarantee an individual's success
  on the job.
- You have created a relaxed atmosphere for the interview so
  you can draw out the candidate's personality.
- You have allowed for self-selection (or self-disqualifica-
  tion) by the applicant.
- You have a good idea of how the person works, based on
  their work samples.
- You have introduced the candidate to other people in your
  agency—even letting those people do some of the interviewing.

You're ready to make a decision.

Step 5: Add It All Up and Make an Offer

"Managers and personnel people feel that they will intui-
tively know the right person when she walks in the door," Joyce
Ross observed. "The masses come in and the managers pick and
choose based on what their gut says. They have a wonderful
conversation, hire the person, and then wonder why they didn't
work out."

I have shown you how to make a careful assessment of the
job and how to find the top applicants. Still, this being the real

world, you probably will not get a perfect fit. Conventional wisdom holds that if you have an 80 percent match between the job and the applicant, it's time to make an offer.

The tools you use to make the decision:

- Use a formal ratings sheet to quantify the information gleaned from your carefully designed interviews. In the first column, list the characteristics you had hoped to find. Beside each feature, rank that person in relation to other applicants and to your ideal.
- Ask everyone who interviewed the person to complete a rating sheet.
- Evaluate the results of your work sample or job tryout.
- Quiz employees who have spoken with the candidate. Knowing your employees as you do, you can get impressions that will influence your decision one way or the other.

But, ultimately, it's up to you.

Make your decision and offer the job to the winner first. If you receive a yes, call the other top candidates *right away.* You don't want them to hear from anybody but you that someone else was hired. This is common courtesy, yes. But the "I'M FIRST" philosophy requires extraordinary courtesy. Thank them for their time and interest, and leave the door open for next time.

Special Concerns for the Public Sector

For those of you in government, my five-step interviewing and selection system may mean opening the door to a whole different way of operating. That door has been closely guarded, and there are many potential difficulties to overcome.

- City or county charters may have to be changed to give you more responsibility for hiring.

- Civil service rules may need to be reformed. Usually, you are given the names of the top three people who have been certified by a central personnel department as being qualified to perform the "process" of the job. You may then select *only* from among the names on that list.
- An independent civil service commission may need to have its considerable power over the selection process curtailed.
- The personnel department is often appointed by the civil service commission and is not accountable to the CEO, leaving you out of the process. This might need to be changed.
- Labor unions may have a say in job specifications, job descriptions, job security, and promotions. This may or may not be helpful.
- The city attorney or county counsel is likely to be very conservative in interpreting public personnel laws. This may inhibit your initiatives.
- There are tight fiscal restraints.
- There are greater needs than in a private firm for consistency in personnel functions citywide. Any change calls for a very strong, top-down commitment. However, the council or governing board is likely to be nervous about any reforms in personnel selection procedures because of a potential public outcry claiming political patronage or favoritism in employment.
- It may take a long time to effect change. On the other hand, your city is only as good as its people. And because government is such a labor-intensive industry, your staff is absolutely critical to your success.

The needed changes are not simple, overnight ones. When I was with San Diego County, we sent charter amendments to the voters several times. We fell flat on our faces—until we won. No, it isn't easy. But *I urge you to make these reforms anyway*. Leadership takes guts, discipline, and—in a bureaucracy—a remarkable ability to stick with an issue over time. The improvement in the way your agency functions, however, will be dramatic. There is no more effective way to build local support for your jurisdiction than to treat your constituents like prized customers by creating a customer-driven local government.

Look to the Future

When your interviewing and selection process works correctly, the people who join your organization will stay there for a long time. The future of your firm depends on whom you hire today.

At Deloitte Haskins & Sells, one of the Big Eight accounting firms, that means examining future markets to see where new business opportunities might be. According to Frank Panarisi, a partner in the firm's San Diego office, the firm identified "the health industry, government, finance, construction, and some industries . . . that are very large but that might be getting stagnant and need help in today's dynamic economic environment."

DH&S then hired people who were expert in those areas, Panarisi said. The market changed, so the firm changed.

Hire for where your company is today *and* for where your business and customers will be tomorrow.

The burden of ignoring the advice will be borne by your employees.

One day I walked into the beautiful suburban branch office of my bank with an unusually large number of relatively small checks listed on five or six different deposit slips. As I reached the teller's window, I implored her, "Please check my addition on these deposits. There are so many small checks here; I'm sure I made a mistake."

The older woman displayed a forlorn look as she said, "When I first came to work for the bank, that was my job. I was here to help the customers and balance the drawer. Now all of that is being done by computer. I don't know what my job is anymore. Now all they want me to do is sell. I wasn't hired as a salesperson, I wasn't trained for sales, and I don't think I like it. I'm very scared."

This woman had been overcome by technology and by changes in the competitive environment. When she was hired, the company did not consider her adaptability for the future. She started out playing one game, but all the rules had changed. She was confused and frightened by the changes—so badly that she blurted her troubles out to me. The bank had failed her, and itself, by not appreciating how difficult it is for some people to make the transition from one set of job skills and self-concepts to another.

It will be costly and time-consuming to retrain this woman to get her back into the mainstream of productive employees. As the situation stands, she may just quit from the frustration, and the bank will have to hire someone else. The employer and the employee both lose.

> **One of the most expensive decisions you will ever make is the hiring of a new employee. So do it right.**

The Ultimate Goal: Responsible Teamwork

"A woman who was seven months pregnant arrived at City Hall at nine A.M. to request a change in the building plans for her new home. She took her number and waited in line for three-and-a-half hours," Joyce Ross told me.

"When they called her number, she was slow in rising from her chair to get to the counter, which was on the other end of the room. By the time she got there, the plan checker said, 'Gee, I figured you weren't here, so I'm going to lunch now.'

"The clerk then closed his window and told the woman, 'You'll have to come back after lunch. You'll lose your place in line because your number has been called already.'"

If this happened in your organization, how would this man's coworkers react? Would they let it slide—"Hey, don't mess with his lunch break"? Or would they take the man aside and say, "That wasn't cool"?

In an "I'M FIRST" company, your carefully selected employees will pick each other up, helping one another to improve their responses to the customer daily. I call this "self-policing." Using my five-step hiring method, you can achieve it, and you will.

6

Reward and Incentive

*"Most people aim at nothing in life and hit their goal with
amazing accuracy."*

—AUTHOR UNKNOWN

I don't believe in statistics. What determines a player's
salary is his contribution to winning—not his statis-
tical accomplishments. Players' livelihoods depend on
their contribution toward the Celtics, not toward themselves,"
said Red Auerbach, the former coach—and current president—
of the Boston Celtics, America's most successful sports fran-
chise.*

Auerbach told how he brought backup center Bill Walton out
of a slump during the 1985–86 season. Walton simply wasn't
scoring. Auerbach told Walton it didn't matter what Walton
scored; all Auerbach cared about was his contribution to the
team. After that conversation, Walton's performance greatly
improved. "He became loose," Auerbach was quoted as saying.
"And he never looked to see what he scored. All he looked at
was: Did we win? And it was 'we,' not 'I.'"

---

*Reprinted by permission of the *Harvard Business Review*. Excerpted from
"Red Auerbach on Management," Alan M. Webber (March/April 1987). Copyright
© by the President and Fellows of Harvard College. Used by permission. All
rights reserved.

People have a normal tendency to "suboptimize": to put the immediate goals and objectives of their own section, department, or division before the corporate objectives. Your production department, for instance, strives to produce each widget at the lowest possible unit cost by using well-known economies of scale. This leaves little time or incentive to do any customized production or short-run orders to solve a particular customer's problems.

Your energy conservation coordinator works to cut the cost of lighting, heating, and air conditioning, and will shut down the building's services soon after 5:00 P.M. The public-contact personnel, on the other hand, want to keep the building comfortable, bright, attractive, and open, to please the customer.

The auditors and attorneys want extensive data and meticulous record-keeping, in order to establish an audit trail. But the marketing, sales, and customer-contact people like to keep paperwork to a minimum so they can spend more time dealing with customers.

Such conflicts are inevitable in an organizationally driven firm. But in a customer-driven company, the priorities are clearer. Customer service is what pushes profits upward, so the firm's reward and incentive system stacks the deck in favor of your customers.

Tie your employees' incentives and rewards to individual, departmental, and corporate objectives—with service to the customer as the main standard.

Rewards Improve Everyone's Performance

Rich Snapper became director of personnel for the City of San Diego, California, in 1979. With an academic background in industrial psychology, he has a long history of involvement with reward and incentive programs. He nicely sums up the payoff executives can expect from a successful reward program: "People rededicate themselves to being high achievers. You can see it; you can sense it: They go out and bust their butts. They appreciate being appreciated, and they work hard. . . ."

After all, says Snapper, "if everybody is treated the same, there's no incentive to be different. *You cannot be a high-performing company if everybody gets a 'C'.*"

If you identify and reward "A" behavior, the standard for what merits an "A" constantly rises as employees strive to attain an identifiable goal. The incentive itself provides an upward pressure on performance. Rewards, then, raise the acceptable level of performance. They elevate employees' awareness of what should be done. Your company is managed more productively.

> **A reward program benefits the employees *and* the company.**

Link your rewards to specific goals and objectives. When businesses consult me about boosting morale and productivity, I often discover that they're plodding toward ill-defined goals, driving a team of unarticulated assumptions. While the managers may have talked with employees about the general nature of the work, and job descriptions may be available, *targeted levels of performance* are uncommon. The workers may be motivated, but they don't know what they're being motivated to do.

Defined objectives and goals are necessary to sustain peak performance over time. The more specific and clear the goal, the more focused the effort.

Recognition—of both outstanding and unacceptable behavior—is more motivating than benign neglect can ever be. The mere act of working with the employee to identify goals and objectives demonstrates your interest in that individual and her quality of life at work. In essence, you are treating her like a customer.

By setting goals, your reward system:

- Clarifies responsibility and accountability
- Directs more effort toward accomplishment rather than "stuff"
- Gives people a concrete reason for working harder
- Promotes originality
- Fosters more precise communication within the organization
- Mobilizes efforts toward finding opportunities rather than protecting the status quo
- Reinforces loyalty
- Identifies nonperformers—to you and to themselves

Performance targeting, with the appropriate monetary and nonmonetary incentives, puts management in charge and gives employees a proprietary interest in the company's customer service mission.

> **Give your employees clear, achievable goals and they will exceed them.**

The Nine Points of a Good Reward System

Below are nine key points that I outline to my clients in helping them set up an incentive/reward system. We'll explore these in detail later in this chapter.

1. Set clear targets.
2. Make the reward fit the goal.
3. Leverage the impact.
4. Celebrate the process.
5. Be personal.
6. Reward what really matters.

7. Include everybody.
8. Shine the spotlight.
9. Create peer pressure.

But first, let's examine some important questions.

Answers to Common Questions about Reward Systems

Imagine that you are speaking to your assembled employees. It could be in your firm's auditorium, at a hotel banquet room, or under a tent at a country club. Excitement and anticipation are in the air. As you begin your award presentation, the room suddenly grows quieter. Then you announce your award winners. The audience groans.

You have lost all credibility: You have chosen people who, as their peers realize, do not deserve the honor. The fear of enacting this intimidating scenario is one reason many of my clients resist providing rewards and incentives in their organizations. Fortunately, the solutions are often easier than they anticipate. The conversation usually goes something like this:

• *"Should I give the reward publicly or privately?"* My answer is that there's no right answer—as long as you do it. Choose whichever way you're comfortable with.

• *"How do I reward people for work that is qualitative— accountants, auditors, analysts, researchers, attorneys, administrators, etc.?"* Here, you have to set your own criteria. Your best attorney is probably the one who gets the toughest cases, so his won/lost ratio may actually be lower than others'. But he's still the best. Forget the ratio and find another scale. Look at the amount of business each person brings in, or the number of clerks he keeps busy on research. In your heart of hearts, you *know* why he is the best. Now, articulate what you already know. Write it down. And reward on that basis.

• *"Should I make the reward available to all or to only a portion of my staff?"* That's a simple one: Everybody participates.

• *"I think everyone in my organization is a top performer—everybody is a 'Ten' or they don't work for me. I can't distinguish among them."* I don't buy that. Even a "Ten" will have an off month now and then. Besides, if they're all great, your reward could be a nickel and they'd fight for it—and improve their performance.

• *"Responsibility and accountability are new terms in this stagnant organization. People will fear my new approach to managing."* No compromise! Give notice that you will start holding people accountable. Take a stand.

• *"There has been no long-range planning here."* I understand. Like many other managerial functions and responsibilities, planning is difficult to do, so it is seen only in the best-run organizations, and is resisted by less accomplished managers. To begin, establish goals and objectives for this month—and incentives and rewards based on them. Now your organization has an immediate plan. Later, you can set up some long-range goals based on this month's discoveries.

• *"We've never even done performance appraisals on a regular basis."* For a reward program to be credible, performance must be frequently and accurately evaluated. Managers who are unaccustomed to or untrained in *constructively* assessing subordinate performance may object to face-to-face appraisals of employees. Institute mandatory, periodic performance appraisals, and train your supervisors to conduct them constructively. Use a simple scale of ratings at first (choices of Disagree, Neutral, or Agree on statements such as "The reviewee presents a professional image"). This will identify problem areas while helping your supervisors get used to the idea of performance review. You can use more sophisticated methods as your appraisers' expertise grows.

• *"Where will I get the money? There is keen competition for resources, both technical and monetary, within my organization. Designing and implementing a reward program will take funds from other projects, costing me political favors."*

I say, *find* the money, *budget* the money, and begin, if need be, with noneconomic rewards (to be detailed later in this chapter). It doesn't have to be cash, as you will see.

• *"Our existing tradition, rules, and procedures compete with this new way of behaving, so a reward program would be criticized and rebuffed."* You know that the rules can't help you the way incredible customer service can. Take charge of your own operation. The customer-driven organization that will win in today's market requires it.

• *"I don't want my poorer performers to be even less productive—to have a disincentive if they are not recognized."* Yes! This is what a reward system does and what it is *supposed* to do. A manager with guts makes it clear who's performing and who isn't. If the poor performers can't take it, they'll find another job. And that's what you want them to do.

• *"Do I reward one outstanding effort, or ongoing, consistent excellence?"* My answer: yes to both.

• *"How do I reward support people whose output or contribution may not be as obvious as that of line production people?"* I make no claims that this is a 100 percent scientific process. Evaluate the role of your receptionists, your maintenance workers, and your bookkeepers, and establish what top performance is *for them*. If you're unsure, ask their opinion on this. We'll see some ways to keep them motivated in the remainder of this chapter.

• *"What form should the reward take?"* There are many kinds. I'll address this question in the next few pages.

• *"I feel uncomfortable talking one-on-one with my employees. I hate speaking formally before a group. How in the world will I get through a reward ceremony?"* It's perfectly all right to be uncomfortable. You can even turn it to your advantage by declaring, "Recognizing you, my staff, is more important than protecting my nerves."

• *"Who makes the decision about who is rewarded—the supervisor, the manager, or colleagues and peers?"* Get input from the whole chain of command. Be very sensitive to what the supervisors feel about their employees' efforts. You may want to set up a panel of executive judges. But ultimately, it's your decision.

• *"How am I going to find the time to do this program?"* Everybody has the same amount of time. I guarantee you will spend the time; it's *how* you spend it that reveals your commitment. To be customer-driven, save some time for this positive step.

Last but not least:

• *"No matter who is chosen for a reward, others will disagree with the decision. This whole program can cause discontent and second-guessing. I'm afraid it will create more problems than it will solve."* My reward system avoids this by being fair, open, and highly focused, giving everyone an opportunity to win the honors.

I tell my clients who voice these concerns that incentives are critical for sustaining the commitment, enthusiasm, and tension required to fulfill the rising expectations of management and of customers. Negativism causes companies to stagnate and become prisoners of their own inertia. Don't let this happen to you!

> **Because your customers' expectations continually rise, you must reward your employees for elevating their performance accordingly.**

Let's go back to the scenario of you standing before the excited crowd at the awards ceremony. If the outcome is a loud groan, as I described, it is because there is ambiguity, concern, and suspicion about what excellent performance really is. Those feelings exist when people have not gotten enough feedback on their performance to know where they stand in relation to others. Their perception of their own performance is inflated. To prevent this, your reward system will be open and unambiguous. Use these nine steps to accomplish this.

Step 1: Set Clear Targets

On February 10, 1986, railroad president Peter Stangl wrote
a memo to all vice-presidents and directors of the Metro-North
Commuter Railroad about his new employee award program:

> The beginning of a new year usually prompts me to take
> stock of the past year's activities and to propose new ini-
> tiatives to improve performance in the year ahead.
>
> We can, I believe, be proud of Metro-North's organiza-
> tional accomplishments and service delivery in 1985. It is
> my intention in 1986 to focus on individuals, especially
> those Metro-North employees whose high standards and
> energetic, dedicated work have singled them out to co-
> workers, customers, or supervisors. I know each department
> has within its work force individuals who consistently ex-
> hibit outstanding performance in customer relations, pro-
> duction, quality control, etc.; or through some extraordinary
> exercise of critical judgment, bravery, or special activity.
>
> To this end, Metro-North Commuter Railroad is estab-
> lishing an employee award program to identify and reward
> such excellent workers.

Spell it out. Let all your managers know what is coming, and
outline the qualities they should be looking for in the award
winners. Then do it!

Here's how:

The goals you give your employees need to be as objective as
possible. Inevitably, there will be a certain amount of subjective
decision-making in the evaluation of performance. To balance
that, set your employees' goals so that they:

* Focus on results and not on the "stuff" of the job. Bypass
  the process and the paperwork, and isolate the reason why
  that person comes to work in the morning.

  Wrong: You must file 400 zoning applications per month.

Right: The customer must receive zoning decisions within thirty days of applying.

- Limit the number of performance objectives.

Wrong: Improve all areas of work.
Right: Submit your reports to the customer within three working days.

- Cover the "big picture" of the individual's job.

Wrong: Make eight sales calls a day.
Right: Improve sales by 10 percent by the end of the quarter.

- Establish a minimum acceptance level and set priorities.

Wrong: Improve reporting procedures.
Right: Reports are due the first Monday of each month. However, if a customer need intervenes, the report will be due on Tuesday by 4:00 P.M.

- Retain flexibility in case unanticipated events or events beyond the employee's control alter the possibility—or desirability—of achieving that objective.

Wrong: No raise if you don't reach your goal.
Right: Goals may be reevaluated in light of unanticipated events.

- Set higher standards than the individual had last year. You're trying to consistently raise the performance level of the individual and the organization, so each objective should acknowledge this.

Wrong: We will maintain customer service as it is.
Right: We will cut product returns by 15 percent this year.

- Finally, each objective must be accompanied by a timetable. No objective should be open-ended.

> *Wrong:* The CSI (Customer Satisfaction Index) will be reviewed regularly.
>
> *Right:* The CSI will be tabulated and reviewed every eight working days.

Step 2: Fit the Reward to the Winner

Salud, Amor y Pesetas, y Tiempo Para Disfrutarlas
(An ancient Spanish toast: "Health, Love and Wealth, and the Time to Enjoy Them.")

Because of the rapidly changing nature of today's work force—in demographics (age, race, sex, ethnic background, religion, etc.), education, value systems, ethics, and orientation toward work—it is essential that you realize that people see things from *their* perspective, not *yours*. Fit the reward to the winner by creating a range of rewards from which to choose. A free trip to Las Vegas may hold no interest for an outdoorsman; offer the option of a hiking trip or cruise, to keep everyone motivated.

A free trip is just one form of incentive. What other forms can incentives take? They need be limited only by one's good judgment, experience, creativity, and resources. Here are examples of possible economic rewards:*

- Award a wage increase without a promotion.
- Make a special "step in grade" pay raise; advance someone one level within their salary range.
- Add a level to a salary range for employees who have demonstrated superior performance.

---

*Portions of the following information on employee economic and non-economic rewards are drawn from *Productivity* (December 1979), published by the U.S. Office of Personnel Management, Intergovernmental Personnel Programs.

- Advance an employee to her next longevity increase before she has reached the usual time in grade.
- Give performance bonuses (monetary rewards that do not permanently increase one's wage or salary). These are usually awarded for specific individual or group accomplishments. *Note:* If the bonus is a $1,000 award, the employee should receive a check for $1,000, *not* for $729.35 because the payroll department took out all the deductions! A reward should be given with *both* hands— not with one hand removing what the other hand has offered. Design the program so that the employee's net cash is a number he can identify with.
- Pay a "premium" rate for work that is above the satisfactory or acceptable level.
- Share the savings. Pass along part of the savings generated when employees raise their unit's productivity. These often are called profit-sharing incentives. The employees' share of the savings can be paid out in cash or put into a deferred compensation or retirement fund. Another form of shared savings goes by the title of "suggestion award program," in which employees whose ideas for cutting costs or streamlining operations to improve performance and productivity are given some part of the savings realized.
- Increasing numbers of employers are funding health club memberships, softball leagues, and social activities as rewards for their employees. This has a payoff for the employer (less absenteeism because of greater employee physical and mental well-being) and it fits with the interests of many of today's employees.
- Employers can offset some of the employees' cost for employer-supplied health insurance, retirement plans, and deferred compensation plans.
- Employers can match funds for employee contributions to nonprofit groups. This is a prestige item for the loyal alumnus or civically active employee.

These are some possible noneconomic rewards:

- Name an "Employee of the Month" and post his photograph in the cafeteria.
- Single the person out in a staff meeting and commend her fine work on a just completed project.
- Consider the options of flex-time, extra vacation time, sabbaticals, and paired jobs. (With the diverse mix of people in today's workforce, their values and needs are more varied than ever before. Certain employees today want more flexible work hours and, increasingly, more time off.) Examples of variations in work hours:

    The most popular version is the ten-four. Employees work the traditional forty-hour week, but they work four ten-hour days, with three days off each week.

    Staggered hours, wherein groups of employees begin their workdays at different fixed times, such as 8:00, 8:30, and 9:00 A.M.

    Flexible, gliding hours. In this system, employees can come to work when they like—within a range of, say, 7:30 to 9:30 A.M.—and work for eight hours.

    Variable hours. Employees set their own time schedule as long as either a predetermined amount of work is accomplished within a set period, or they work for a predetermined amount of time.

- Have a department head buy the employee lunch or dinner.
- Create a special parking place for the Employee of the Month. It's his for one month.
- Throw a testimonial dinner or luncheon.
- Issue formal citations of merit.
- Create special emblems, badges, or uniforms for distinguished employees.

- Put the employee's name on the door of the truck he drives, proclaiming his worth as an exceptional performer.
- Display a special emblem on the patrol cars of outstanding police officers.

Step 3: Leverage the Impact with Style and Timing

Give the reward as quickly as possible after the successful performance. You want to strengthen the employee's association of the intensity of hard work with the joy of the reward. In contrast, rigidly scheduled annual bonuses can delay exceptional performance until, say, the eight weeks before review time (or 16.7 percent of a fifty-two-week-year). "If a person knows that he or she will be reinforced after a fixed period of time for acting in a certain way," University of North Florida professor Robert C. Ford and Burroughs Corporation executive Ronald Couture wrote in 1978, "he or she tends to lose interest in acting that way until the time for reinforcement approaches.

"Having all employees paid on the same payroll dates may be convenient for data processing and the personnel department, but it may be totally inappropriate for helping the trainer or foreman show the new employee the relationship between desired behavior and financial reward."* One good quarter per year won't make it in today's customer-driven market. Keep the rewards coming.

More about style: When you make a cash award, give a permanent remembrance as well, such as a letter or plaque. Why? Your employee will take the check, put it in her bank account, and in time, the impact of the reward might dissipate. But the accompanying letter or plaque will be a constant reminder that renews the good feelings that came with the reward.

---

*Robert C. Ford and Ronald Couture, "A Contingency Approach to Incentive Program Design," *Compensation Review* (1978). Copyright © 1978 by American Management Association. Used by permission. All rights reserved.

Step 4: Celebrate When You Become Number One and While You Are Becoming Number One

When he headed the Boca Raton Hotel and Club, Ted Kleisner used a mix of economic and noneconomic rewards. He worked to create a family feeling among his employees and managers. In chapter 3, I described the Thanksgiving dinner he gave for his staff and their families.

"We also have a couple of other functions that we throw. Everyone has a picnic—that's nothing new—but we have Olympic games during the picnic."

The workers form five teams and "there are a lot of baloney events like a team cheering contest to see who can come up with the most creative enthusiastic cheer for their department." The hotel pitches a big tent on its driving range for this event. Again, families are invited.

Throw a picnic. Run some races. Take everybody out to the nearest lake for swimming and recreation. Have fun at these award programs. Celebrate being number one, and make fun of some of the natural tumbles you will experience in becoming number one—as long as forward movement occurs.

Step 5: Make the Reward Process as Personal as Possible

Los Angeles County Sheriff Sherman Block handles his reward system personally. "For example, last year, we promoted one hundred seventy-five new sergeants. I had a lunch with every one of those sergeants," he said. "Not one at a time—ten, twelve, fifteen at a time as they were promoted. But I do have a lunch with every person that's promoted in the department, to congratulate them on a one-on-one basis. I also pose for a photograph with them with their new badge."

At these lunches, Block talks to the officers about their new role. "I try to impart information that I think they're going to need to carry out their responsibility, *and* I solicit comments from them."

Step 6: Reward to Reinforce Your Corporate Values

Customer-driven companies use their reward and incentive systems to reinforce their value system and nurture a positive corporate culture.

Set criteria beyond bringing in new business and accomplishing projects on time (or ahead of time!). For example, Deloitte Haskins & Sells feels that the client is buying integrity and loyalty when he hires DH&S. That means community involvement. Accordingly, part of the DH&S bonus and reward system is tied to employees' involvement in community service activities.

Individuals who work with such agencies as the United Way and groups that aid the homeless "do a better job for the client," Frank Panarisi asserts.

"Our company is interested in people and the well-being of others, not just in being accountants or consultants. I think that reflects that we're good people and good people to do business with. . . . Our commitment to the community says to our clients: Our people know you. Our people know your company. Our people know your community, and the environment you're living in."

Step 7: Include Everyone—Stakeholders Are Profit-Makers

At Sewell Village Cadillac in Dallas, Texas, the customer is number one. A large part of that philosophy comes from Phil Dunnet, who as service director oversees all of the dealership's fixed operations—jargon for the service and parts departments.

Sewell Village employs about 240 people, and is the largest Cadillac dealership for 1,000 miles in any direction. In 1985, it sold 3,050 new cars and 1,500 used ones. In 1986, despite the recession that hit Texas oil, sales totaled 2,500 new cars and 1,100 used. According to *Automotive News*, Sewell Village is the largest fixed-operation retailer of cars, service, and parts in the United States. Businessmen and women from around the world make the pilgrimage to Dallas to study Sewell Village's management methods and reward systems.

How did Sewell attain this position? "The philosophy is that we, number one, want to reward our winners," Dunnet said in talking about the dealership's incentive system. "The best way we know how to do that is on a performance basis. We have very few salaried employees around here. Anytime I can 'incentivize' someone, I strive to do that."

For Dunnet himself, "There is no salary at all. I am paid on a percentage of net profit. If I do not generate a net profit, then I don't get paid. In fact, I end up owing the company if my net profit is a loss. So I have a very strong incentive to make this thing work."

Such "share of net" deals are fairly common in the automotive industry. What is unusual about Sewell is that this kind of incentive is extended to *all* the employees. Consider these three examples.

First, the Institute for Automotive Service Excellence and General Motors sponsor certification programs to recognize the industry's top technicians. At Sewell, those who become certified are paid a $1,000 bonus. These "Master Techs" are permitted to wear white shirts on the job as part of their uniform; the other mechanics wear gray. Now, that is a visible symbol of reward that gives the other workers something to strive for.

Second, each man's work station has a plaque bearing his name and the date that he started at Sewell. Around the border of this plaque, Dunnet said, are stickers like those given to college football players for outstanding plays. The technicians win stickers by being tops in service. Dunnet compares the system to the World War II aces who would paint a swastika on their planes for each Nazi plane they shot down.

I asked him if these plaques are seen by customers or just by the men's peers. "They're seen by as many tours as we send through here," he replied. "We had AT&T this morning, we have Nissan this afternoon." That kind of recognition is hard to come by for most auto mechanics.

A third incentive at Sewell Village directly involves the treatment of customers. At a typical dealership, a customer service representative is a guy like "Fred." After the customer pays his bill, the cashier gets on the public address system, yells out a job number and: "Fred! Gogitit! Fred!"

"Then," said Dunnet, "ol' Fred gets up off his stool and saunters back there and gets the car. He turns the radio up good and high and brings it on up."

"Screeches it on up," I corrected.

"Oh, absolutely! He has to make up for the slowness of his gait on the way out, so he has to drive like hell to make it look good," he said.

Around Texas car lots, such people are known as "lot lizards." Sewell Village has driven the lizards out and replaced the P.A.'s blast with a computerized set-up that gets the customer's car to him faster. The employees who use the system are paid X amount per car brought up. In addition, the employee with the top total each week gets a $20 bonus—not to mention bragging rights for a week.

The procedure: The cashier punches the relevant information—job number, parking space number of the car, etc.—into a computer. Over where the "lot lizards" *used* to lounge, this information appears on a computer screen. A customer service rep then types in his initials to tell the cashier that he is the one going out to get that car. No noisy intercom here, and the system is interactive, to boot. Seeing the initials, the cashier can tell the customer, "David is bringing your car up, sir." It's a personal touch that comes via computer.

"And that starts the clock," Dunnet said. The clock stops when that customer service rep returns with the car and punches back in on the computer. The cashier asks the customer to hand the computer printout to the person who brings his car up. This completes the circle, giving the rep his documentation for the weekly reward.

"We count the number of cars they bring up," Dunnet said, "and we count how fast they bring them up. . . . Now, instead of somebody sauntering out to get the car, you'd better look out because [our guys will] run you over. They are definitely motivated to move quickly."

At Sewell, *everyone*—from the top guy to the mechanic to the former "lot lizard"—is on an incentive system.

> **Include as many people as possible in your incentive and reward system.**

Step 8: The Spotlight on Good Performance Makes Poor Performance More Glaring

Sewell Village's technicians are paid by volume—but there are plenty of assurances that top-quality work is being done there as well.

Dunnet gave me this example: "You bring your car in and say, 'I need my air conditioner serviced. It's April, and it's going to get hot here soon.'"

Sewell adjusts the machinery, does a performance test, and makes sure that "everything is up to snuff. Then, sometime in early May, you get ready to use your air-conditioning system and it's . . . just blowing hot air."

So you bring it back to Sewell, saying, "What's the deal?"

The service adviser apologizes profusely and sends your car back to the person who worked on it the first time. "And that technician would be made to make the repair at no charge," Dunnet said.

"Number one, the technician would not receive any payment for doing it over again.

"Number two, while he is doing this work at no charge, there are other jobs coming into the shop that he is unable to work on because he's doing this no-revenue job."

With a reward on the line, it is *always* in the employee's best interest to do the job right the first time.

> Your reward system can reinforce top-quality work and make poor performance more glaring.

If an employee can't meet the standard, he'll try harder—or give up and quit the job. Not everyone is suited to the customer-driven future. But if you use this kind of reward system, the cream of the crop—the ones who thrive on challenge and all-out participation—will stick with you.

Step 9: Build in Peer Pressure

A major component of Sewell's reward mechanism is a system of posted grades for each employee. The "leader board," designed to showcase those with 100 percent error-free work, is posted by the service reception driveway, which is near the lunchroom as well, so everybody sees what everybody else is doing.

All the technicians start the month with 1,000 points. If quality control inspectors return a job to a technician to be redone, points are cut from his score. But the inspectors also can issue a "pat on the back" for exceptional work, which cancels out a rejection.

In the lunchroom itself is a bar chart showing each individual's score.

"They sit there and eat lunch and say, 'Hey, turkey, how come I'm at 993 and you're at 940?' It's a pretty good incentive," Dunnet said, "to make sure that they do it right."

> Posting of results builds peer pressure and appreciation into your reward program.

Fight to Get In, Sweat to Stay In

The all-encompassing reward system I have outlined exerts a constant upward pressure on the quality of work produced— pressure from peers, from self-interest, and from employees' internal drives to be number one. What may have been good enough to win last year is earning the technician only third-place honors this year. As more and more white shirts replace the gray ones, the gray-shirted mechanics will feel more and more uncomfortable. They will work harder to make the grade, which strengthens employee loyalty and commitment.

"Organizations that do not pay well are doomed to become the training ground for those that do!" asserts Rodney Cron in his book, *Assuring Customer Satisfaction* (New York: Van Nostrand Reinhold, 1974). "It should be a place where people 'fight' to get to work there and—once in—'sweat' to stay."

Recognizing this upward spiral of performance, Manpower Temporary Services in San Diego calls its reward system "Can You Top This?" At regular staff meetings of all fifty-five employees, the top five win $50 Nordstrom gift certificates. The award winners are chosen on the basis of laudatory letters from clients or coworkers detailing the superb job that these employees have done.

One recent winner arranged to have a book showing the spectacular sights of Hawaii waiting in her client's hotel room when the client arrived for her first visit to the Islands. This coffee table book gave the client and her friends the perfect preview of their vacation. The thought behind the special effort was "You're a special customer and I want your vacation to be extra special, too."

"People look at these stories, and talk about them, and say, 'Can you top this?'" Manpower's Mel Katz told me. "It's a great way to get our people to think about service."

It's no coincidence that agency owners Mel Katz and Phil Blair chose a visit to Nordstrom as the currency of their prizes. "We want our people to go there and see that type of service," Katz told me.

The reward systems I have outlined will keep your employees' morale up through tough times and keep them around in good times. Why should they leave your firm when they are already making good money and their work is appreciated? There's a challenge awaiting every employee in this vibrant workplace.

I once won an award that was very special to me because I had worked very hard for it. I have since won other awards. But that special prize still gives me a sly little smile when I need one. That smile has lasted many years. Put some of that confidence on your employees' faces. When they see their buddies' new suits purchased with bonus money, they'll know you're serious about customer service. And when they're wearing *their own* bonus-money suits, you will have helped them pocket that long-term smile.

7

Support

"Impossible dreams are often achievable because nobody else tries them."
—SALLY REED, COUNTY EXECUTIVE OFFICER,
SANTA CLARA COUNTY, CALIFORNIA

On the last day of his life, twenty-three-year-old Richard James Callahan (not his real name) picked up his son at two o'clock in the afternoon for their weekly two-hour visit. Because he had beaten up both his wife and her father, the courts had prevented Callahan from seeing the three-year-old for any longer than that.

Callahan's estranged wife usually left the boy at her mother-in-law's house and waited there for Callahan to bring him back. (The courts had also prevented Callahan from having any contact with his wife, according to police and press accounts of the day.) But on this Sunday, Callahan didn't bring the boy back. Instead, he called his mother's house and demanded that his wife meet him. He told her that if she called the police he would kill her, the son, and any police officer who intervened. He told her that he had a friend's gun.

Callahan called the house several times, saying, "I'm going to call you again in five minutes, and I'm going to tell you where I'm going to be. I want you to go there, and I'll bring the boy with me." He repeatedly asked her not to call the police.

After the second or third such call, however, she did exactly that. Assistant San Diego police chief Norm Stamper was on duty that day. He was a lieutenant then, and, as he recalls it, he went with a sergeant to interview Callahan's wife. She described the gun to them as a .32-caliber pearl-handled revolver.

According to Stamper, she related some other things that Callahan had done that had led to the court order forbidding him to talk to her or see the child for more than two hours a week. "She also told us that he had threatened to kill anybody who attempted to intervene," Stamper told me, "and that he would kill his son and kill her.

"We left her under the protection of another police officer," Stamper said. Then he, the sergeant, and other plainclothes officers organized a search for Callahan. "We had a car description [and] a description of him and of the son."

Stamper and his sergeant spotted the car in the North Park area of San Diego and followed it for a dozen blocks before Callahan pulled in at a gas station. "In the meantime," Stamper said, "we had put out the word that we had the car in sight and that the father and son were in it."

Callahan was headed for a pay phone inside the service station when Lieutenant Stamper came up behind him and identified himself as a police officer. Callahan ran.

Stamper chased him, calling out for the man to stop, saying that he was a San Diego police officer and that he wanted to talk to him. Meantime, the sergeant arrived at the passenger side of Callahan's car, where the boy was sitting, but the door was locked.

"Callahan jumped into the car," Stamper said, "grabbed his child, and screamed repeatedly at the top of his lungs, 'I'm going to kill him! I'm going to kill him! I'm going to kill him!'

"He circled the child with his left arm and motioned with his right hand, then stuck his hand up against the child. . . .

"I couldn't see whether there was a gun in his hand. . . .

"I took out my service revolver, and from a distance of about twelve inches, shot Callahan in the head."

Seeing blood all over the inside of the car, the sergeant believed that Stamper had been shot, and he started firing. "I yelled at him to stop," Stamper said. "I reached in, pulled Callahan's body out, and just dumped it on the ground. I got the kid in my arms, who was splattered with his father's blood. This little tow-headed kid. He was crying, of course, and completely covered with blood.

"I gave him to a detective who had pulled up in another car. They rushed him to a hospital. He, fortunately, had not been struck by bullets or glass. Physically, he was OK. Homicide rolled up shortly after we reported this. The sergeant and I were separated, as is policy. We were not allowed to make statements to each other." (The responsibility of officers involved in a shooting is well known. The men are separated, and each writes his own report before he talks to *any* other person about it.)

Stamper was put into the back seat of a police car, and no one talked to him. "Knowing and understanding the policy, I was not bothered by that in the least," he said. "I was driven to police headquarters. The sergeant likewise was driven by another officer to police headquarters.

"My service revolver was taken away, which of course is policy. And I was asked to write a report of what had happened. I sat there in my blood-stained shirt—I still remember, it was kind of a peach-colored shirt—with blood on my shirt, blood on my pants, blood on my shoes, and I wrote a police report.

"After finishing the report, I handed it in and went home. I never talked to anybody about that incident after that. That was it."

Stamper was twenty-eight years old at that time.

"By the time I got home, I felt that I had—believe it or not—really worked it out, that I understood what had happened, and that I could deal with it," he says today.

He felt that, beyond explaining to his wife what had happened, he "did not need to talk about the effect it had on me because I wasn't feeling any effects."

Stamper had been teaching at the police academy for several years when the shooting occurred. He told young recruits that, while they must be proficient in the use of firearms, they also must understand the "terrible responsibility that goes along with the decision to shoot or not to shoot." He also told them that it is extremely unlikely that an officer will *ever* fire his weapon in the line of duty. Having reached the rank of lieutenant, Stamper recalls that he felt surprised that at that relatively late stage of his career, he had drawn his firearm and killed a man with it. "It was a very intellectual process. The emotional stuff was clearly there, but I was not in touch with it.

"The only people who spoke to me about it, and this was in the several days immediately following the incident, said things like: 'Nice job.' 'Nice shot.' 'Gee, our resident intellectual really is a cop.'"

He received a letter from the district attorney a few weeks later, clearing him of any charges related to the killing and commending him for his quick and brave actions in saving the three-year-old's life.

A reporter who had written an in-depth story on Stamper before the shooting sent him a note: "Knowing you and your feelings about guns and violence, I know how you must feel."

"But we didn't talk about it either," Stamper said. "I didn't talk to anybody."

The organization did "nothing at that time to prepare people for these kinds of incidents," Stamper said. "Worse yet, there was no mechanism to help people work through something that must be worked through." (Emphasis mine.)

Today, the San Diego Police Department sends a *peer support officer*, also called a companion officer, out whenever there is a shooting that involves police. The police officer involved is still isolated from other witnesses, but the companion officer is present, "steadfastly avoiding any discussion of the tactics or the shooting policy or procedures. Rather, [he would] spend time with the officer talking if that's what the officer wanted, listening if that's what the officer wanted or needed," Stamper said. "Generally, [he would] be there to offer psychological support."

When he is summoned, it is the campanion officer's responsibility to the department—and to his fellow officer—to proceed immediately to the scene, whether he is on duty or not, day or night. This is one way in which the San Diego Police Department now supports its employees. (The program was begun in 1982—ten years after Stamper killed Callahan.)

The peer support officers are very carefully selected. They receive the best training in providing this emotional support. This training is ongoing. They are all volunteers for this assignment, and have qualified for it the hard way: Each one has experienced a "police-involved shooting" from close range. Each, in effect, has sat at headquarters, writing that same report, with blood on his shirt, blood on his pants, blood on his shoes.

What Is Support?

Your employees cannot respond to your customers as you want them to unless *you create* systems that support responsiveness.

Support means giving your employees respect and responsibility. It means providing psychological, managerial, technical, physical, and professional backing. It also means providing the potential for economic security. (Notice that I didn't ask you to *guarantee* economic security. You provide the opportunity to earn top wages; the employee must respond to it.)

Unless you run a police department or other security force, your employees probably will never shoot anyone in the line of duty. But one of these traumas, or something like it, is more likely to happen to you:

- An armed robbery at one of your retail outlets
- A fatal crash involving a company vehicle
- A crippling accident on the production line
- A leak of toxic gas into your office building

- A decision to close a factory, laying off thousands of employees
- An employee who loses a child

"Support," according to Chief Stamper, "is based on the concept that *in any line of work* . . . there are predictable traumatic experiences that individuals will undergo. A universal need when human beings are subjected to trauma is to process the experience—to think it through, talk it out, come to an understanding of what's taken place, and consider where one goes from here.

"If I do not deal with the emotional aftershock," Stamper continued, "I either start or add to a process of becoming rigid . . . of sealing myself off. . . . [I] become less flexible, less sensitive to what is going on. I begin to lose that intuitive edge. . . .

"So when I put my mind to work on the challenge that I'm facing, or the decision that needs to be formulated, the outcome is not going to be nearly what it could be—perhaps should be— because of that limitation."

What systems does your company have to support an employee who faces such a traumatic experience? Are they informal or haphazard? Do you follow a "least said, soonest mended" policy, or does your agency help the employee recuperate emotionally (and, in the process, recoup your investment in that employee)? Crisis aside, what are you doing to support your staff day to day?

When I lead seminars for customer-contact employees, I am often asked to respond to this question (or something like it): "Linda, what we have been learning here is dynamite! However, I'm responsible for answering fourteen telephone lines. Three days each week I also cover the front counter. I have no backup. When I'm constantly being run off my feet, how can I treat customers as if they come first?"

My answer to this employee is, "You can't."

My question to you, the manager, is, "Are you inadvertently making it impossible for your employees to do what you say you want them to do—and train them to do?" If so, you are losing credibility, wasting money, and frustrating your staff.

Install a new telephone system, redesign your schedule for covering the front counter, increase (or reassign) your staff. The investment is worth it!

Eight Categories of Support

1. Sensible rules and policies that work to the benefit of the customer
2. Personal respect and fairness, promoting responsibility plus accountability
3. Psychological and emotional—including *fun*
4. Managerial—committing the necessary resources and the people
5. Technical—providing new equipment for new jobs
6. Physical, the safety factor
7. Professional—helping employees grow
8. Economic—creating the potential for financial security

Category 1: Don't Let the Rules Get in Your Way

Rules have a way of multiplying and assuming a life of their own. Rarely are procedures and policies instituted with sunset laws attached to them—provisions which mandate that the policy will automatically cease to exist within, say, one year unless it is specifically renewed.

Hence, your employees end up carrying a back-breaking load of policies on their shoulders. That load can slow them down, leaving them sluggish and bewildered by the size of your rulebook. In order to form effective customer relationships, workers need to be supported, not weighed down.

Your policies, rules and regulations should be user-friendly: convenient and effective from the customer's point of view. They should be viewed by employees and customers alike as encouraging good relations, not constraining them.

In my seminars, I ask customer-contact workers to tell me the three company policies that most frequently prevent them from satisfying customers. I then ask the employee to explain to me (as if I were the customer) the *benefit to me* of that policy.

People who participate in this exercise realize that they have no idea of the rationale behind the policy!

Let's say a zoning administrator is forced to deny an application for a sign that a shopowner wants to erect in a local shopping center. The permit for the sign is denied because the planned sign does not adhere to the size requirements mandated by the city (usually the sign is too big). The shop owner is furious. He argues that he needs a sign that size to attract people to his store.

If the zoning administrator had been given the proper support by management, he would be able to explain to the store owner that the city's sign ordinance (regulating the design and size of the sign) benefits him because it fosters a certain ambience and consistency of quality throughout the shopping center.

The worker would point out to the owner that these regulations are designed to create an upscale environment. This attracts customers with more disposable income. Those people will spend more money in the shops. Because the signs are uniform, they will feel that they are in a safe, contemporary environment, thereby cutting down on rowdy clientele and vandalism. That will keep the owners' insurance rates lower while simultaneously promoting a high-end customer base. The zoning administrator would point out to the shopowner that property values tend to rise when there is a quality environment—and that kind of environment is promoted by consistency in design.

Ideally, this is what would happen.

Typically, however, the individuals participating in my seminar cannot come up with these valid, clearly justifiable reasons during our discussion. "Because the city wants it that way" is as far as many of them get.

> You want a minimum amount of rules. For the rules you do have, your employees must be able to explain to the customer how each rule benefits that customer.

When there are too many rules to observe, some inevitably will be ignored. That is hypocrisy, and the company loses credibility in its employees' eyes. In my seminars, I recommend that you have a minimal number of rules along with a very, very strong culture and value system.

Some firms are using this theme to advertise that they are customer-driven. "The SECURITY FORCE"* is how Security Pacific National Bank described its staff in a 1986 advertisement in the *Wall Street Journal.* The headline read: "We understand your needs, but they are different from our rules," and is signed, "Some Banks."

A second headline reads: "There's every reason to be flexible." The ad is signed: "The Security Force in San Francisco."

According to this ad, "the SECURITY FORCE" understands that flexibility and responsiveness to the customer are more important than "the rules." *Reevaluate your rules* if they are getting in the way of customer service. This is a crucial way of supporting your employees, who must enforce the rules that deal with the customer.

> The customer-service attitude is determined (and maintained) by the culture, not by the rules.

*Copyright © 1986, Security Pacific National Bank. SECURITY FORCE is a registered trademark of Security Pacific Corporation.

Category 2: Personal Dignity and Respect

We know that people tend to live out the expectations other people have of them. Therefore, the more professionally your customer-contact personnel are treated, the more professionally they tend to behave.

I know of a car dealership that has instituted a system of customer satisfaction follow-up telephone calls. But the leadership is diluting this well-intended effort, because the calls are being made after most of the staff has gone home by a part-time receptionist seated at the switchboard. Amid receiving calls and taking messages from customers whom she has never met and knows nothing about, she makes the customer feedback calls.

She does the best she can under the circumstances, but an organization's least-trained, part-time employees should not be the ones following up with customers. This dealer cannot make good on its commitment to customer service because it is not supporting its employees to help them meet customer service goals.

To support your customer-contact people—be they salespeople or filing clerks—I recommend these steps:

• Discuss professional attire and establish standards. It may be coat and tie; it may be a clean, crisp uniform; it may be the proper protective shoes. Set a standard for your employees so they will know what image you want them to project.

• Ensure that the physical environment is conducive to effective and efficient work as well as being inviting to the customer. Eliminate loud P.A. systems, intrusive phone bells, ventilation drafts, and sloppy piles of paper or other supplies.

• Give all customer-contact personnel business cards, as you do with other professionals in your organization, as well as desk nameplates and/or name tags. The goal here is twofold: First, to enhance the perception of polish and professionalism both for the employee and for the customer who is interacting with her. The more personalized the interaction with the customer, the more the customer feels that he is dealing with a human being who will be responsive rather than an unnamed, uncaring bureaucrat. Second, by having everyone identified by name, you enhance responsibility and accountability. It makes it much easier for the customer to get back to the same person, so he doesn't have to explain the problem from the beginning every time. It also makes it easier for management to trace unprofessional behavior.

• Treat customer-contact personnel with the same prestige, incentives, rewards, salaries, and so on as you do other marketing and sales employees.

• At all times, inform them fully of company policies, rules, procedures, plans, and changes in plans. Few people in your organization better understand what your customers want, what upsets them most, and what they will pay good money for. Therefore, customer-contact workers' ideas and feedback should be taken into consideration at all policy levels and planning meetings. They should be in on company retreats, sales conventions, strategy sessions, product and service development, and brainstorming. (A full discussion of how to glean employee feedback appears in chapter 4.)

Coaching Instead of Punishing

Former San Diego police chief Bill Kolender used more counseling and fewer "by-the-numbers" punitive measures to achieve his customer service goals and provide support to his staff.

For example, reviewing officers will talk to a citizen who has complained of excessive force during an arrest. They also talk to the officer. They then evaluate the facts. Kolender contends that this procedure is atypical. The public sector usually goes by the numbers:

• "You do this, you get two days' suspension."
• "You do that, you get four days' suspension."
• "You do this, you get a reprimand."
• "You do that, you get fired."

"That does not build a competent, stronger employee," Kolender said. "That tears down and makes the employee weak and bitter."

The question is "Are you focusing on reprimanding someone for doing something wrong? Or are you focusing on 'How can I correct the behavior? How can I make that person a better employee?'" In each situation, Kolender continued, "we evaluate the facts and the person.

"If management says, 'You closed the door when you shouldn't, you're suspended for a day,' the employee says, 'Thank you very much, I'll see you later.'

"What have you got when they get back?

"You've got a very bitter employee."

Work to correct the behavior, not just to punish it.

Category 3: Psychological and Emotional Support

Step 1. *Start with trust.* Mario Arrigo, general manager of Villa d'Este on Lake Como, Italy, supports his personnel through "personal relations." That means that any employee can walk into Mario's office at any time to discuss business or personal problems. This kind of faith and trust is essential to the support relationship. So make yourself approachable. Eat in the company cafeteria with your employees regularly to provide encouragement and support and to symbolize that you are available. Play in the company golf tournament—and not with a foursome of other executives. Get out and deal with the people.

Step 2. *Expect a lot, give a lot.* You want everyone to feel that his or her job is important. That belief comes from an attitude of mutual respect among your staffers. Furthermore, you're setting the example. If you ask for a commitment of long hours, but disappear promptly at 5:00 each evening, you're undermining your own efforts. Employees will see through that in no time, and their goodwill erodes.

Step 3. *Do things that boost your employees' self-confidence and self-image.* This will make them more outgoing and more interested in building customer relationships. Ed Florign, former general manager of the Vista International Hotel in New York City, brought in experts to talk to his staff about investments, stocks, and banking. Standing in the heart of the Wall Street financial district of New York City, the hotel draws much of its clientele from that industry. Florign wants to demystify the terminology his guests use and, in the mind's eye of the staffers, to transform the bankers into human beings.

Step 4. *Capitalize on the "mint factor."*

Jack Terhar of Sill-Terhar Ford in Denver, Colorado, is considered a national leader in the automotive industry, serving on the Customer Satisfaction Committee of the National Ford Dealers Council. His dealership consistently wins top honors from Ford for its customer service performance. Because the customer service elements enumerated below *are important to its employees*, Sill-Terhar Ford provides them. This kind of internal support for your staff is highly visible to your customers as well. The list: mints, balloons, a car wash. A cashier wanted to give mints out to people when they paid their bills, as is done in fine restaurants. *"She loves giving mints*, and it makes her attitude better," Jack said. "And it makes the customers smile at her. It's one of the things that just changes an attitude between her and her customers and makes her a little more proud of what she does." So the dealership supplies the mints.

When a car is sold, the dealership sends a *"bouquet"* of *balloons* to the buyer's workplace. If it is a working couple, both wife and husband get a bouquet. "You can't walk through an office where someone has a big bunch of balloons without saying, 'Oh! Who sent you those?'

"And on goes the conversation," Jack said, noting that the answer is, "My car salesman sent me these!"

Anchoring the balloons' ribbons are some of the famous S-T

Ford mints for the lucky buyer to share with his coworkers while they smile and talk about how great Sill-Terhar Ford and its salespeople are.

The balloons make the job fun for the salespeople, too. Jack estimated that seven out of ten customers call the salesperson to thank him or her for the balloons. A few phone calls like that and the salesperson is pumped up. "It changes their attitude," Jack said, "and makes their job more fun." It lifts their self-esteem and sends them out to sell with total confidence and commitment.

"The service personnel felt that if they were going to change their image, it was very important that *every car get washed*," Terhar said. The dealership bought its own drive-through car-wash, and the work areas are kept clean, too. The customer's perception is that the car was not only repaired, but renewed.

Step 5. *Work to overcome their fears*. "A lot of people are afraid they can't do something, but they don't necessarily tell you that. You have to be sensitive enough to know that they are scared to death of something and really pump them up," Ira Gottfried, a general partner in Coopers & Lybrand, told me.

"Maybe that's through role-playing, or maybe that's through telling them how you would do it and then having them feed it back to you. It's emotional support. It's what you do with a child, truthfully, and then you push him out into the cold world and let him do it.

> "You have to let them make their own mistakes. But *you* pick the mistakes."
> —Ira Gottfried, Coopers & Lybrand

"You don't send a new person to your best client and let her screw up. You send them to a smaller client to learn how to handle things, and then a bigger client and a bigger client. You bring them along."

Category 4: Managerial Support

Using your employee survey (see chapter 3), you can deduce what your employees need from their supervisor, manager, and/or the organization to do a better job servicing their customers—whether their customers are internal or external to the company. Here are six steps to take in providing managerial support:

Step 1. *Listen to your employees' suggestions.* Phil Dunnet of Sewell Village Cadillac in Dallas, Texas, gets good results by responding quickly to employees' ECRs. An ECR is an *Error Cause Removal* form. The form begins: "I have discovered a problem that is preventing me or my coworkers from doing our job right the first time." Then there is plenty of space to describe the problem.

A quality improvement team (QIT) meets weekly to review, among other things, the ECRs that have come in. That team is made up of:

- Dunnet, the company's fixed operations director, who is in charge of the service and parts departments, the body shop, and the dealership's cellular phone department
- A technician
- A financial/administrative person
- The service manager
- The parts manager

It's a mix of "some of the department heads and some of the real players," Dunnet said. "We attempt to close out the ECRs within a week," he said, "so we can give the employees feedback on what we're doing to make it better."

Properly used, feedback from your employees can guarantee that the first time is the right time. The ECR form allows every employee every opportunity to be successful because it removes obstacles from their path. So if an employee is screwing up, there is no one at fault but himself—and everyone knows it.

Step 2. *Make authority clear.* Always have someone available to the staff who has the necessary authority to handle problems that other staffers are not authorized to deal with. This eliminates delays for the customer and embarrassment for employees over their inability to handle a problem. Everyone needs to know who the next person is up the line, and how to reach her.

Step 3. *Be available and visible*. You should be accessible, influencing and reinforcing employees, and encouraging them to help one another. Realize that most employees do not move freely around the organization, the building, or the office because their jobs do not give them the time. Managers' jobs do. Take advantage of this.

Visiting the outlying locations and different work shifts in the organization, as well. June Hendershot of Great American Savings & Loan told me the story of the time when she and Jim Schmit, then president of Great American (now vice-chairman of the board) were driving to Orange County from San Diego on business, and scheduled their drive so that on the way north they visited no fewer than seven Great American branches.

Step 4. *Back up their decisions*. "First of all, Linda, *anybody in the dealership*—from the cashier on up—can give *anything they deem necessary* to the customer," Jack Terhar said. "I have total faith and trust that they're going to make a good decision. They can make a decision at whatever level, and provide whatever service they see fit to provide to the customer at that particular moment, in whatever magnitude necessary.

"If the cashier decided to give somebody a new car because the customer was totally dissatisfied with his car, I would give the customer a new car.

"I'm not certain that the cashier and I wouldn't sit down and talk about it [later] and discuss whether it was the right or the wrong thing to do, but there would be no chewing out about it or anything else because I have confidence that these people can make those kinds of decisions."

More often, Terhar said, the cashier uses less dramatic means to defuse disputes. She might reconcile a customer's unwillingness to pay a $78 bill when the estimate was $75 by knocking off the "extra" $3. But "it might be $50," he added.

"It might be any amount." If she felt that it was the right decision, Jack accepts it.

Contrast this attitude with a more typical story from Ed Etess of Web Technology: "I've been to stores where there might be a five-dollar dispute," he said, "and they kept six people in an office, spending an hour on it, and it must have cost them two hundred dollars over a lousy five bucks. The hell with it, OK?"

Step 5. *Back up your words with resources.* In talking with me about what it takes to create a quality company, Etess observed, "Once you establish the quality-of-performance guidelines, and you establish the priorities [as we have discussed in previous chapters], then you have to do a staffing analysis. Here's where you get the difference between a quality company and one that's not.

"A quality company will see whether a quality job can be done with the people on staff and still meet those guidelines and priorities. If it can't be, they'll hire more people.

"Talk is cheap," Etess said. "If someone says, 'We want to respond very quickly to our customers,' or 'We want to get our orders out the same day they come in,' management should then ask, 'What does it take to get something out the same day?'

"Well-managed companies will find the resources.

"If you tell your staff, 'Do whatever it takes to satisfy the customer,'" Etess said, "management shouldn't put the salesperson in a conflict between the company and the customer. . . . Avoiding that conflict can mean something as simple as having the right forms available to your employees. Don't penalize your staff by making them fill out a twenty-minute form so they can't sell something to another customer and get a commission." Examine your order forms. Do they make things easier for your employees, or do they slow things down? Do your policies and procedures help or hinder your staff in serving your customers?

Step 6. *Encourage employees to ask for help.*

"All of us at one time or another have put our foot in our mouth and caused a problem," said Ira Gottfried of Coopers &

Lybrand. "I certainly have a long list of them. I want my people to recognize when they've done that. They should come back to me and say, 'Look, I am in trouble; somebody come and rescue it before it gets worse.'

"I have fired probably half a dozen people over the past twenty years who were in trouble and did not come yelling. I have never fired someone who got into trouble and called out for help. Early warning of problems is an obligation of a professional. You can usually rescue the situation if you know about it early."

Category 5: Technological Support

Sometimes a simple technological tool will help you ensure employee productivity. When you bring your car in to be repaired at Sill-Terhar Ford in Denver, Colorado, the person who writes up your order gives you a beeper.

This beeper improves service for you, as I'll explain. But it also functions as a support mechanism for the dealership's employees. "When the beeper goes off," Terhar explained to me, it signals "the customer to call the dealership . . . We immediately put the technician on the phone with the customer so that the two of them can communicate directly . . . to assure that the repair is done properly."

Terhar used the example of a brake job. The technician has pulled the car into a service bay and, after checking it out, sees that it needs a brake job, which costs $120. He goes to call the customer for a go-ahead.

"He has both wheels off, he has spent maybe thirty minutes tearing the car apart," Terhar said. "If he can't get in touch with the customer, he has one of two choices. One is to let the car sit on the rack until [he gets] hold of the customer. That's lost time. That doesn't make the technician happy because he's not making money. Two, he can put the car back together and push it outside, which means that it moves to the back of the line. The employee loses the work, at least for that day, and it messes up our scheduling. And the customer's car doesn't get finished that day because we had no way of contacting him. We were really creating a lot of problems by not being able to contact the customer.

"The beeper was a very simple way to correct it, and very inexpensive."

> **As a way to support your employees, see their jobs from their point of view. Look for ways to keep your employees working.**

The salespeople at Sill-Terhar Ford also get strong backing from the dealership. Each salesperson is responsible for calling the people to whom he has sold cars—twice a year for five years. He receives bonus money for making these calls, regardless of what the customer-satisfaction results are.

"If they make the call," Terhar said, "they will be more than able to keep the customer satisfied. *The critical thing is that we maintain contact with that customer.*" Because after you've bought one Sill-Terhar Ford, Terhar wants you to buy another one.

The dealership supports the salespeople by keeping a computer file on each customer, and printing a list telling the salespeople which of their customers are due for a call that month. Based on the age of the car, the salesperson might bring up specific "service recommendations that could prevent the customer from having a major failure down the road," Terhar said.

"We feel that the call itself is so important because if the customer has a problem, they will normally tell us.

"Just making sure that the contact is made," Jack said, *"takes care of the majority of the problems."*

This computerized system evolved from Terhar's past as a car salesman. "I did a very good job of follow-up," he said. But he had trouble keeping track of everyone and finding the time to mail them follow-up letters. "I feel it's important that each customer not only receive a letter but also a phone call. A phone call [alone] is not as good as a letter *and* a phone call," he said. And so the computer also is used to address and print out the letters, which are then signed by the salespeople.

Thanks to the computer, the dealership's salespeople can be tops on follow-up—and all they have to do is sign the letters.

"When a salesperson leaves our dealership," Terhar said, "either the new person coming in or some of the old people in the dealership take those customers and continue to follow them. Those customers never feel that they lose contact with the dealership. Therefore, we increase our chances of selling them their next vehicle."

Maximize your staff's value to you and to your customers by finding new technological ways to help them.

Category 6: Physical Support

Criminals grow bolder. Medical expenses soar higher. Insurance companies demand new safety measures in exchange for lower premiums. These and other factors contribute to your employees' need for physical support, which I define as protection of their safety and health.

How does your firm measure up to this checklist on the elements of physical support?

- Security guards who limit access to your offices, and who can escort workers to their cars at night
- Well-lighted, well-ventilated offices, corridors, and stairways
- Functional fire-fighting equipment and fire extinguishers, and regular fire drills

- First aid and CPR training provided by the firm
- Life and health insurance coverage
- Correctly maintained company vehicles
- Consistent safety rules
- Where appropriate, emergency plans and drills in case of flood or earthquake

There are no real surprises on this list; they are fundamental elements of the professional work environment you are trying to create. Firms that are lacking in this area have a very basic philosophical problem to resolve before they can become customer-driven. I hope you passed the test.

Category 7: Professional Support and Career Planning: Feedback for Your Employees

Even the most technically adept person will not necessarily do the quality job you want him to do if you don't train him how to do it. As I often tell my audiences, "People are only as good as they know how to be."

Among the ways that Deloitte Haskins & Sells supports its employees are career counseling and ongoing performance evaluations. In DH&S's career development program, management sits down with the employee and talks about the person's career plan. "They work with an adviser on identifying strengths, weaknesses, and where the individual would like to go in the future," Frank Panarisi told me. "The next step is to find out what the firm can do to help the individual.

"We want people to develop to their optimum because they'll be better producers for the firm," Panarisi said. "We want to keep them excited about growth and opportunity. That enthusiasm will reflect on the firm and on the clients."

Another major component of DH&S's support system is the firm's use of frequent and in-depth performance evaluations. *After each assignment*, the manager of the project evaluates all the consultants who worked with him. As with any performance appraisal, the results are discussed with the employee by the project manager.

This immediate feedback to the employee has a double benefit: (1) It gives the successful individual praise and reinforces optimum performance; and (2) it points out areas where the employee can improve.

Deloitte Haskins & Sells uses another powerful support tool called the Exceptional Management Program. It is not a traditional evaluation, but rather an assessment of the individual *by his subordinates*. An outside personnel firm queries a manager's subordinates and interprets the data to reveal the manager's strengths and weaknesses. The manager and the outside firm then set up a plan of action for improvement.

When I asked Panarisi who reviews the employee's plan for improvement, he replied, "No one else approves. . . . It's a personal thing."

He admitted that these reviews can be "kind of devastating to the ego." To soften the impact, the managers meet in groups of six. There is a general discussion of how to interpret the information the consultant is providing. Then the managers can share with their peers their impressions of their individual ratings. They may reveal as much or as little as they like.

This is the purest form of support. Consider:

- The firm pays for a review of the manager by her subordinates.
- The information is gathered confidentially.
- The results are compiled and evaluated confidentially.
- The manager's plan of action is developed confidentially.

There is only one purpose for this program: the individual's self-improvement. This kind of counseling can be crucial to an employee's success. If your employees are successful, you are, too.

Category 8: Provide the Potential for Economic Security

Sewell Village Cadillac looks out for its people by keeping them productive. If they're not working, they're not earning—for themselves or for Sewell.

"Let's say we have three technicians who specialize in air conditioning," Phil Dunnet said. "And here it is, February. 'When are we going to use our air conditioning in February?' the customers think." But when the air conditioning specialists are not working, they are not getting paid. "They're sitting on the bench and becoming very forlorn," Dunnet hypothesized.

"We need to do something to help those fellows out. So we'll say to the service advisers up front, 'Let's sell air conditioning performance checks, or heating system performance tests, to help these guys out.'

"That solves two problems: We help the service advisers by giving them an incentive [for something to sell] and to break up the monotony. Two, we give the air conditioning technicians something to get them off their bench and onto the floor and working."

Here are examples of two other forms of economic support:

• Joe Turner, human resources director at Home Federal Savings & Loan, described to me the *employee emergency loan program*. Under it, any employee can borrow up to $300, to be paid back through payroll deductions, at only 6 percent interest. Joe said that Home Federal never loses money on these personal loans, and the firm defines "emergency" very loosely.

• Jack Terhar makes a point of *recognizing the worth of the "support personnel"*—the clerks, cashiers, and receptionists who handle the administrative details of the dealership. "We used to use our receptionist and our cashier positions as training positions," he said. "And then, in our infinite wisdom, if they were really good, we promoted them into jobs for which they were not as well suited. Now I have one receptionist who is paid higher than a big portion of the people in my office because I feel that it is a key position. . . . [The receptionists] talk to more customers than anybody else in the dealership does." Terhar pays these workers accordingly, even if it goes against the traditional value placed on other job titles.

Compensate your staff according to the value they contribute, not according to their job title alone.

Sill-Terhar Ford supports its people strongly so they can do the kind of job Jack Terhar wants them to do. The beeper system gives the technicians (and the dealership) bigger incomes. The computerized customer-tracking system cuts down on the salespeople's wasted time. *Realistically* valuing each employee helps each to serve the customer and the organization more effectively. And the "mint factor" keeps them smiling.

John Singleton of Security Pacific Corporation and Security Pacific Automation Company, Inc. (SPAC), told me this story about the support system at his firm—and the difference it made in one woman's life. "Our reputation," he said, "is that we're not the lowest-priced, we're the best quality. And Security Pacific people go the extra mile. They'll work all night, all weekend, to get your work out. They do that again and again."

One staffer had told him that day that she had had half an hour's sleep the night before because she was getting a job out for twenty customers—and she was on her way to a class in graduate school that day! That is the "kind of attitude we want our people to have," Singleton said.

"She was a secretary seven or eight years ago. [Now] she's probably a $55,000-a-year person finishing her degree, and we're paying for it. The reason she's in school is that we made her go to school. We convinced her that she really ought to go. . . . We literally said to her, 'If you want to be in a position someday where you're competing against a man and he has a degree and you don't, and you allow some person who's biased—not here at Security, but maybe somewhere else—to choose the man, that's wrong to let that happen to you.' She knew we were right, and now she's in a graduate degree program."

SPAC took responsibility for this employee's well-being and career advancement. Now she is earning a hefty salary *and* an advanced degree, and all of her considerable energy and skill is focused on the company and its customers. *Supporting your employees supports you.*

```
┌─────────────────┐
│                 │
│       8         │
│                 │
└─────────────────┘
```

Training and Development

"Your employees are only as good as they know how to be."
—AUTHOR UNKNOWN

I t was a public meeting of the San Diego County Board of Supervisors, during the annual budget hearings. As usual, many interested citizens were in the audience, eager to hear how much money the board would allocate to their pet programs. The front rows were filled with TV cameras, radio reporters, and writers from the county's major and suburban newspapers.

The five members of the elected board of supervisors sat on a dais. Key executive staff members were also present, including me, the deputy chief administrative officer. This was the first time in several years that the county was attempting to create a significant, central pool of monies for employee training countywide. I was there to defend that fund.

The board members were questioning me about the program, as is standard procedure. A member of the board of supervisors addressed me: "Ms. Goldzimer, I do not see the necessity of training the county staff. By definition, when we hire someone into a position, they are deemed to be qualified to fulfill the obligations of that position. They should begin to perform competently in a very short time. They don't need any training. And I, for one, do not intend to vote any money for this purpose."

I fought the urge to come back with, "If they are so well-prepared and confident, why aren't they paid more?" I did, however, argue, "How can members of the staff be expected to assume higher levels of responsibility if they are never exposed to new attitudes, values, skills, concepts, and ideas? Without training, our employees will be obsolete!

"Management has an obligation to the staff to provide personal and professional development. If we don't train our employees, they will be surpassed by the competition and the information we give our customers will be antiquated. What is the value of our most expensive and basic resource, the human beings who work here?"

In a *San Diego Union* article, Tom Peters reminds us that "the $30-billion-a-year corporate training bill of U.S. companies looks impressive at first. But it is a small fraction of our annual corporate hardware bill of about $400 billion. Our training spending, only 75¢ per employee per day, is a pale shadow of the training commitment of our most fearsome competitors, such as West Germany and Japan."*

I wish I could say that my experience that day was atypical in private or public organizations nationwide. Sadly, it is not.

The labor force is the most expensive asset in most companies. Help them make a state-of-the-art contribution to your success!

You maintain your car so it can get you where you want to go.

You buy equipment to speed your computer operations.

You enlarge the capacity of your phone system.

Why not sharpen the capability of your employees through training?

As the seventeenth-century French playwright Molière said, "It is not only what we do, but also what we do not do, for which we are accountable."

San Diego Union, October 19, 1987. Copyright © 1987 TPG Communications. All rights reserved.

Connect It to the Customer

"I know what I should do, but I don't know how to do it," is the frustrated cry of many employees in today's businesses. When I talked with Peter Stangl, president of the Metro-North commuter railroad, which serves New York and Connecticut, he told me, "The worst thing you can do is ask someone to do something that they're not capable of doing. They get scared."

When that happens, the employee might try to hide that lack of confidence with some exaggeration or deception. Stangl said, "Most people are afraid to come up and say, 'Hey, I can't do this. You've got to help me, you've got to train me. I am not capable.'" If employees receive any training, it is usually in the technical part of their jobs—how to operate the earth mover, run the press, or fill out the forms. They are rarely told about, much less trained in, the people component of what they do.

Organizations mistakenly assume that if a person has an outgoing personality and good technical skills, he also has the ability to anticipate customer problems, dissipate the anger of an irate client, create a "golden handcuff" with the customer (making the customer so attached to your firm's goods and services that he can't get away and buy from someone else), and expand repeat business with the customer. They haven't realized that without specific training and staff development toward these ends, the bonding necessary for continued customer satisfaction is left to chance. Customer service skills are *acquired* skills, just like learning to use a word processor or a cash register.

The waiter who makes a brusque remark, the sexist who alienates an executive at your client's firm, the stockroom clerk who says, "We only have three hundred and you can't have all of them" to a customer seeking 2,000 car parts—all of these people need training. They don't realize that their true job title is "customer service professional." With training, you can give them a wider range of responses to use in customer interactions.

A sample of the "how-to" skills needed within a customer-driven company:

- How to build a relationship based on trust
- How to convert an angry customer into a satisfied one (we talked about this in chapter 4)
- How to turn a negative situation into an opportunity for more business
- How to create a bonding relationship when you can't see the person—as is the case on the telephone

When your staff is highly skilled in these areas, productivity will increase because *they'll be doing things right the first time.* They won't have to repeat their words, redo their work, or check as often with their supervisors and their customers.

Training in these skills can manifest itself in many ways. In Nordstrom's famous shoe department, for example, my brother bought a beautiful pair of soft, Italian leather Bruno Magli shoes in deep maroon. When he was paying for them, the salesperson selected an appropriate shoe polish and casually tossed it into the shoebox. My brother came home thrilled about having gotten something "extra" (free and unexpected). A really memorable little touch.

When I had occasion to talk to the general manager of that store, I asked about it. "Rick," I said, "what is the Nordstrom policy on giving away free merchandise?"

Rick replied, "We don't give away free merchandise, Linda."

I told him the shoe polish story. His response: "We probably received the shoe polish on a special promotion from Bruno Magli, but we handled it so that the customer feels special, unique, and important—as if we were doing something especially for him."

Have your employees been trained to think this way? Can they come up with such inventive "extras" on their own? The importance of such skills becomes even more apparent when you realize that employees at all levels rarely are fired or not promoted because of deficiencies in *technical* competency. It is usually because of people or relationship problems.

When Money Becomes an Issue, You Must Take a Stand

Sally Reed is county executive of Santa Clara County, California. Her training program includes a "customer awareness" component that has had immediate results. (I know, because I designed and implemented it.) How can she justify that expense to her governing board, citing demonstrated, quantifiable benefits?

"You probably can't do that very well," Reed said. "The question you ask yourself is 'If I could do what I really wanted to do in county government, what would it be?'

"A lot of chief executives get caught up in wanting to do 'real work'—put together a communications system or a redevelopment contract or something concrete, because we deal in so many abstractions. . . . I dared to set goals for myself like improving the county's image and building pride in the organization."

During budget hearings in June 1984 (again in full view of reporters, local TV cameras, and an audience), Reed faced a challenge. The board of supervisors had reclassified her training money from the Yes list to the Maybe list. She would have to speak out to protect her commitment.

With her staff, she developed a short presentation. She planned to talk about the heavy investment that the best companies make in training, and how much other counties were spending. Just before the hearing, however, she looked at this list and tossed it aside. Her speech, she told me, went like this: "'The board knows what this training effort means to me. It means pride in the organization, it means changing the way every individual feels about it. It means . . .' and I went on like that for five or ten minutes.

"They put it in the budget."

Sally Reed didn't say to her elected public officials, "This expense will save you 8.345 cents per county resident." The cost of the training will be recouped from savings in employee turnover and reduced absenteeism. The main thrust of her argument to the board was her commitment to her employees and to building their commitment to the county and its customers.

What Is Good Training?

In any training program that I do, my first priority is that training should be *fun*. Unless the environment for learning is relaxed, comfortable, and enjoyable, the participants simply are not as susceptible to change. I relate anecdotes, I smile, I encourage questions and comments. I want my trainees to feel that they're a part of the process.

What other elements should be present? Consider the following list:

• Empower each employee with enough skills to achieve positive results with customers. At the same time, recognize the limited resources that employees often must work with, and acknowledge that many customers will be continually difficult.

• Break your material down into manageable increments so that people have a chance to master prerequisite skills before they are faced with more complicated ones.

• Be sure that all participants know the answer to "WIIFM" ("What's in it for me?"). The instructor must be able to establish for each participant the positive, direct impact of this training on her life, her profession, her needs, and her desires. How will this training benefit her as an individual? Don't assume that because people have been sent or have volunteered to participate in some form of training experience that they truly understand how it will benefit them. In my experience, the trainer must make the connection crystal-clear.

• Target the training to your company's specific needs, goals, and objectives. I don't believe in "canned" training, or delivering the same seminar for any two groups, regardless of the special interests of the audience. Predeveloped videotapes, workbooks, and films are valid teaching methods only when they are part of an individualized package that includes discussion and exercises. But they are a waste of time when used alone. Training that is custom-designed is the most effective for the money spent.

When my firm designs a training seminar, we first send the client a ten-page questionnaire that asks questions such as:

What are the demographics of the group?
What are the major issues or problems facing your industry, your company, and this department?
Who has "trained" these people before?
Who will speak to them afterward?
How does this program fit into the larger scheme of strategies, goals, and objectives of your company?
What do you want us to accomplish as a result of the training?
What are the major achievements of this group?
What are they ashamed of?
What are they troubled by?

This questionnaire is followed up with either an in-person conference or a series of telephone conferences between the trainer from my company and key representatives of the client firm. Additionally, I request a plethora of reading material from the company, the department, and the industry. This includes in-house newsletters, trade journals, bulletins, and so forth. *I read them all* before I meet with the trainees. That way, I can design a program that is targeted and focused, using examples that are pertinent to my audience to demonstrate my points.

The trainer's material must fit your staff's specific circumstances.

• Give the trainees some tangible, take-home material that serves to reinforce the training, such as resource books or workbooks. A fun catch-phrase that's easy to remember will help remind them of the thrust of the lessons. Put it on a button, bookmark, or sticker.

• Keep it simple and basic—even for the most sophisticated issues. People easily experience information overload. The more complicated the procedures, recommendations, or ideas, the more the trainer guarantees that they will not be put into practice. Furthermore, a good trainer will build on what is already familiar, accepted, and well known to the trainees.

• If people are going to learn, they must practice. This practice should take place in a safe, positive environment where people feel confident about taking the risk of trying something new. Try to compliment every effort. Find something right in what people are attempting to do even if the end result is wrong. Then coach for a better result.

• Recognize and celebrate the new proficiencies that result from the training experience. For example, consider implementing an informal or formal accreditation program. Create a system that recognizes—much like a college diploma—when an intern becomes a resident, when a law clerk passes the bar exam, when the accountant becomes a CPA, when the bank teller has finished teller school, when the typist reaches the ninety-word-a-minute milestone, when the analyst has mastered some new software on your computer, when the section accomplishes zero product returns in seven days, or when the unit receives at least four compliments from customers per week. The message? "We care enough about you to invest in you. We care enough to give you the opportunity to invest in yourself. Aren't we a great partnership?"

As Zig Ziglar, the famous motivational speaker and trainer, says, "I develop employees as I mine for gold. I may have to move three tons of dirt to find three ounces of gold, but I don't go into the mine looking for dirt, I go in looking for gold."

Train the Managers, Too

The environment that the trainee is returning to within the company must be supportive of the skills, attitudes, values, and behaviors he has just learned.

One of the most expensive and silly mistakes that companies make is to expose people to training, and then send them back to an unchanged workplace. You have spent a lot of money and time creating a training experience that has altered behavior or thinking in some positive way. But if the other people in the office or factory don't change at all, what will happen? Naturally, old habits and old ways of doing things will choke out the new, and nothing is accomplished.

Therefore, it is *absolutely essential* that from the first-line supervisor upward, your managers know what's going on during the training experience. Help them devise ways to reward, reinforce, and support the new behaviors.

Training Takes Many Forms

Make a list of what comes to mind when I mention staff training or staff development. If you are like my clients, you will write: formal seminars and workshops, usually conducted by a "professional trainer." But there are many ways that you can train your employees every day. My concept of training encompasses these eight methods:

1. Daily supervision
2. On-the-job training
3. Playing the part, or self-training
4. Mentoring and war stories
5. Cross-training
6. Classroom training
7. Analyzing the competition
8. Progressive discipline

These eight forms can be combined in whatever way is most suitable for your organization and best helps your staff to serve your customers.

Daily Hands-on, Supportive Supervision

I also call this coaching. It means showing the employee the right technique, then letting him try it. In their classic book, *In*

Search of Excellence (New York: Harper & Row Publishers, Inc., 1982), Tom Peters and Bob Waterman coined the now commonplace phrase "management by walking around." "Walking around" also provides a two-way training opportunity. The executive who is "walking around" has an excellent chance to find out what is really going on in the organization—and who is doing it. So *he* is being trained. Additionally, while talking with his staff, he can impart his vision and the mission of the company directly to the employees, so he is training *them* as well.

On-the-Job Training

Mario Arrigo, general manager of Villa d'Este, says, "The only way to learn a job is to do the job. In the U.S.A., you have training programs and seminars. We don't do that here. Here, our supervisors are very close to the worker, and you learn while you're doing. Also, here we have a very large span of control. Our department heads do not have assistants. We are just the managers and the workers. Consequently, we really see how well our employees are actually doing the job with the customer."

A more day-in-the-life example: I had a very limited time to get to the airport, check my baggage, park my car, and make my cross-country plane. Of course, I had not left enough time for any of that, let alone to secure traveler's checks before my long trip.

When I am experiencing one of these days, I tend to become very agitated and aggressive. Such was the mood I was in when I walked into my local branch of Great American Savings & Loan. I was greeted with a friendly smile by a teller who, I soon surmised, was in training. She was inexperienced at issuing traveler's checks, and was taking longer than I would have wished even under the best of circumstances. I asked if there was someone else who could help me, as I was in a great hurry. Noticing the teller's—and my—building anxiety, the assistant manager came by.

Showing great confidence and support in her teller, she gently guided and expedited the transaction, never interfering with the work being handled by the trainee. Although making it clear to me that the bank was doing the best that it could, this manager's unfailing goal was the development of her staff. She stood by, reassuring me while allowing the trainee to successfully complete the experience of working under pressure, learning the ropes, and serving the customer.

This performance as an effective coach/supervisor has stayed with me for many years. It would have been very easy for her to take over the transaction in order to satisfy me, or to hang back and allow the trainee to become increasingly frustrated and nervous. Instead, she took the hardest but most effective choice. She allowed the trainee to continue handling the transaction; reassured me, the customer; and provided backup support that facilitated the transaction. Most importantly, this manager gave the trainee the confidence needed to serve the customer (and all future customers) well.

With that kind of base, that teller has a much better chance to succeed, personally and professionally, and prove a valued asset to the bank.

Self-Training

Self-training boosts your employees' confidence. When a developer turns up with his high-powered entourage—architect, lawyer, engineer, personal assistant—to deal with a $30,000-a-year plan checker, the transaction is set up for the planner to be intimidated.

Once your employee is intimidated, it's natural for him to:

- Hide behind the rules
- Want to be right
- Want to "win"

All of these can interfere with the real task at hand. To overcome these tendencies, the planner must cultivate an image of confidence. If he will *act* as an equal, he will be *treated* as an equal. I call this self-training.

For Ira Gottfried of Coopers & Lybrand, this attitude is the "polish factor." It includes good grooming and dress as well as coaching in the art of small talk. And perhaps a little make-believe. The clients coming to Gottfried's consultants are often chief executives, so he strives to give his consultants "an executive presence." He wants them to be seen as equals by the clients.

"Today, I make as much money as my clients," Gottfried said. "I belong to a country club, I drive a Mercedes, and I am equal. But there were many, many years when I drove a cheap little car and had a cheap little house. But I dressed right and I made believe. I role-played that I was comfortable and wealthy and equal. It may not have been true, but my customers believed it."

Mentoring and War Stories

At Coopers & Lybrand, everyone is assigned a mentor, and part of the mentor's job is to coach his pupil. "Hey, you need a haircut; go out and get one," the mentor might say.

The mentor will also accompany the pupil on a presentation—ready to rescue the project, if need be, otherwise just taking notes on things to discuss back at the office. Gottfried recognizes that not everyone can play this role. "Once you have appointed mentors, you need to keep a close eye on the relationships . . . simply because the chemistry is not always right. If it doesn't work out, you are going to have to switch mentors."

War stories, too, have an important place in training. After a round of golf or a dinner with a big client, Gottfried will discuss with his people what was said, along with the little, humbling details that show them that the CEO of the client firm is just a human being like you or me. He says he is a war-story teller. "The more recognition I have [among my staff] that the people they are doing business with are as human as they are, the better they will be able to deal with them.

"War stories pay off."

Job Rotation and Cross-Training

This gives the employees a wider exposure within the organization and a better appreciation of their coworkers' roles in serving the customer. New waiters, for example, should spend a few nights in the kitchen, helping the kitchen staff and chefs, before ever waiting on tables. Likewise, have your supervisors drive a delivery route for a couple of days every few months. They'll come back from the experience with new and better ideas on how to do things—and a greater appreciation for what can go wrong.

Assign your designers to the production department for one month a year. Saying "Do it this way" from a building a quarter of a mile away seems to be much simpler, but it is far less enlightening to a manager seeking improvements than actually doing it with his own two hands.

Take your employees who deal with the product after it's been made and put them at the other end of the production line. Besides giving your employees new insights into their own jobs, this exposure improves cooperation, communication, and coordination within the organization.

On-Site and Off-Site Formal Seminars and Workshops

These may involve using either in-house trainers or outside expertise. Selecting the right instructor is crucial to winning the desired advantage. The best instructors are those who make it a point to know your industry (or who come from your industry). They are role models in their own right, and they have the ability to *show* people how to do the job rather than do it for them.

Too many times, I have seen companies make instructors or trainers of those people who are temporarily at loose ends in other positions and need something to keep them busy and make them look productive. The results can be disastrous.

Beware of the paradox of selecting an instructor who is excellent at what he does but doesn't know how to instruct, and vice versa. For example, I have seen far too many police departments award the critical position of field training officer to someone who may be excellent at patrolling the streets but who hasn't the foggiest idea how to transmit those instincts and skills to a new recruit.

Comparisons with the Competition

Visit competitors' firms and/or use their products and services. Look at the competition from your customers' point of view. For example, it is commonly said that if you drive down the street in Detroit, you would never know that the United States had big competition from Japanese cars. Why? Because nobody in Detroit drives a Japanese car! But if you don't get out there and see, touch, and feel what your competitors are providing to the market, you are not in a position to compete and win. All of this is part of training. Stay at other hotels as a guest, eat at other restaurants, and wear your competitors' shoes.

The manager of a five-star hotel told me, "Guests from the United States are very particular about their rooms, particularly bathrooms. Space and size is an important element to them, whereas the Japanese do not have the same expectations [regarding] size as do people from the U.S.

"How do we know all this? From our experience. People who are successful in this business have made it a point to put themselves in their customers' shoes by being a hotel guest. You must travel a lot, all over the world. You must know the country of origin of your guests in order to accommodate them well." No wonder this hotel has been such a success for so long!

Correct Honest Mistakes Instead of Punishing for Them

"People are trying to get the job done. . . . Maybe they lack a certain competency. Maybe they're good police officers who have had a bad day and they make a mistake." So said Assistant Chief Norm Stamper of the San Diego Police Department. What these officers needed was training, not a slap in the face. And Stamper developed a new discipline system to accomplish that.

When Stamper was reassigned from administrative services to head up field operations in 1983, he spent about three months working on the streets and in the station houses with line officers, getting reacquainted with procedures. He found that the streets had changed in the six years he had been away. Within the force, much of the paperwork was the same. But he saw what he described as "an extremely unfair system of discipline."

"We did not discriminate between honest mistakes—or poor performance—and willful misconduct," Stamper said.

Stamper and fifty other officers redefined discipline as *esprit de corps*, as morale. "They suggested that discipline involves education and training, and *building* the organization. Not tearing it down," Stamper said. He examined 100 of the department's 355 files on its formal disciplinary actions for 1983. Those cases included offenses such as:

- Police car accidents
- Knives left on prisoners (missed during a search)
- Being late for court dates
- Being late for work
- Use of excessive force
- Discourtesy to members of the public
- Ignoring standard procedure

The fifty officers said they felt that the existing system actually was creating and encouraging dishonesty—both among officers and among their superiors. "Officers would hide their transgressions, knowing that they would get nailed for them," Stamper said. "Supervisors who felt that the disciplinary system was unfair would overlook even the obvious need to intervene in the work of their officers to correct poor performance.

"Since they felt they could not administer a *corrective* form of discipline—coaching, counseling, a poke in the ribs, a raised eyebrow, sending somebody to school—without being perceived as being soft or irresponsible, they simply overlooked the minor transgressions."

Working with police captains and commanders—the police department equivalent of managers—Stamper rewrote the discipline manual and created the concept of a "bifurcated" disciplinary system. In this system, a deputy chief in charge of personnel hears each case and decides which part of the bifurcated system will apply: the retraining section or the punitive one. This chief makes the distinction between poor performance and willful misconduct.

This is much like the system used in many states for lawbreaking motorists: They are sent to traffic school. After a certain number of lessons, the offense is removed from their driving record. Re-education—not a fine—is the consequence of bad driving.

Is your organization more interested in punishing errant behavior, or in *improving* it by coaching and counseling? Do you swat the child on the behind, or do you show her that she shouldn't touch the stove because it is hot and she might burn her fingers? Your employees shouldn't hesitate to act for fear of being second-guessed and chastised. If you want them to use their time most effectively, train and retrain when you see a need for it. Top customer service requires it.

The Tale of the Untrained Plumber

I'll wind up this chapter on training with a true story that shows how a person poorly trained in customer relations spoiled a firm's best technical effort.

The plumber was working in my house. The sink was fixed, but the kitchen floor was left muddied and wet. When I asked the plumber to clean the floor, his response was sullen and begrudging. Cleaning the floor wasn't his job, he said.

I didn't care that the water now flowed fully and freely through my sink. My floor was filthy! When I think back on this customer transaction, the only thing that I remember is my dirty floor. That company has lost my business forever—and all of my friends have been warned about them, too.

Train your employees "to fix the sink" (the technical part of their job) *and* "to wash the floor." That way, they will leave a lasting, positive impression that strengthens your relationship with that customer. Training is the secret of cost-effective staffing and a cornerstone of customer satisfaction.

9

The Intelligent Loss of Sales

Y ou may run a tight ship. Your people may be well trained in helping the customer. But until you have a functioning "I'M FIRST" system, you risk confusing your employees and losing your customers.

As a final example that ties it all together, I want to tell you about the Price Company—"the original cash and carry warehouse"—and introduce you to Sol Price, the firm's chairman and founder.

The Price Company did $1.283 billion in sales in the last *quarter* of 1987 at its Price Club stores in California, Arizona, New Mexico, Virginia, Maryland, Connecticut, New Jersey, and New York. Profit on those sales was $30.8 million. (And this was the quarter of the October 1987 market crash!) They must be doing something right.

Sol Price's operation illustrates that really knowing who your customer is and *designing your business from that customer's point of view* translates into profits of the kind that most businesspeople cannot even imagine. Price contends that long-term success derives from "the intelligent loss of sales."

"There are some customers I don't want," he told me in a meeting at his San Diego headquarters. "There are some sales I don't want. I don't feel the need, if I have Clorox, to carry Purex. And I don't feel the need to have the gallon and the two-gallon and the half-gallon and the pint bottles. I select the thing that I want for [my] niche of the business. Let everybody else have the other customer."

The message: Do not attempt to be all things to all people. That is impossible. Start with knowing *your* customer. Then create, design, deliver, implement, produce, distribute, and finance to fulfill the needs of *that* market niche. The Price Club is as closely attuned to its customers' needs and desires as Nordstrom is to its more high-end, upscale clientele.

Adopting the Customer's Point of View

"I think you can be a good merchant by seeing yourself through the eyes of your customer—and being a very critical customer," Price told me. "Obviously, you've got to decide what the hell it is that you're trying to do. Are you trying to be a Nordstrom? Are you trying to be a Price Club? Are you trying to be something else?"

The business started in 1976 because Price and his partners "perceived the need for cash-and-carry warehousing to service the small businessperson who was no longer an attractive customer to the manufacturer or distributor because . . . he didn't buy enough."

Price sees his customers as coming to him because his stores:

- Offer them quality merchandise at very low prices.
- Do much of the selection for them. "Although we have a broad variety of merchandise, within a category we have a very narrow selection."
- Make it easy for them to do much of their shopping in one place.

- Make it fun to shop there. "Price Clubs have become kind of like bazaars," Price said. "They are not only a good place to go and save a substantial amount of money, but apparently, it's fun to go there . . . because of the enormous variety of goods in a relatively small space." It's akin to an Easter egg hunt for adults. "There will be some tires, and right next door to the tires you might find some potted plants," Price said. "Next to them you might find some Dom Perignon champagne."
- Allow customers to feel a sense of ownership. The Price Club is truly a club—you have to be a member to shop there. Membership is open mainly to businesses, though individuals affiliated with certain credit unions and banks may join.

Today, a Price Club is a big warehouse. Heavy-duty metal shelves reach almost to the ceiling of the three-story, 100,000-square-foot building. Everything comes in the large, economy size: four dozen chicken drumsticks in a freezer bag; a three-pound can of coffee; a bundle of ten notepads; a box containing four dozen cartons of cigarettes; eight rolls of 35-millimeter film in one package. Each store carries 3,500 different items—no more, no less.

After hearing him talk about how a firm must "constantly be looking at" itself from the customer's point of view, I asked Price to describe the relationship that the Price Club—with almost no sales help, and its goods displayed in a hodgepodge, warehouse environment—has with its customers.

"Well," he said, "there is the relationship when you go to Bergdorf Goodman and there is a clerk there who knows you. And she says, 'Oh, Ms. Goldzimer . . .' That's one kind of relationship."

At a Price Club, the relationship revolves around the membership card and the bazaar-like quality of its stores, where a discovery is around every corner. Because of this fun factor and the membership, Price said, "The customers feel it's theirs."

The Six Rights That Right All Wrongs

In Sol Price's philosophy, the customer's image of your organization comes from three elements that she *sees:*

- Your building, its fixtures, all the grounds around it—and perhaps your fleet of vans, your crackerjack mail-order fulfillment system, or your user-friendly instruction books
- Your merchandise
- Your people

To each of those elements, six criteria are applied. Price said, "We call them the Six Rights." They are:

1. The right kind
2. In the right place
3. At the right time
4. In the right quantity
5. At the right price
6. In the right condition

He integrates the Six Rights into every aspect of his company. For example, "The right kind of employee in the back room in receiving might not be the right kind of employee doing the cashiering," he said. This corresponds to my own advice to clients that they hire a who, not a what. For cashier, he chooses the kind of person who enjoys the stimulation and pressure of assisting a long line of people. The receiving department is quieter, with a more orderly atmosphere, requiring someone who prefers that kind of environment.

Applying the sixth right, "in the right condition," to merchandise, Price said, "It might be a great piece of merchandise, but because of the way it was handled on the floor, it gets banged up. Now it's in the wrong condition." Condition affects the image of the company—which we discussed in the chapter on integration.

"For instance, [consider] a sign. Is the sign in the right place? Is it in the right condition? A lot of merchandisers will post signs that contain more technical knowledge for *them* than information for the customer."

As a customer-driven company must do, Price looks at every aspect of his physical plant: "The toilets—are they in the right condition? Is there paper in there? Is the floor wet? Is the floor dirty?" How does the customer see it?

The third right is timing: "Are you trying to sell Christmas paper in February?" That won't work. Sell it when the customer needs it.

The fourth right is quantity: "Have you got too much merchandise? Too little?

"The same principles apply with people. You can have too few people, you can have too many people. You can have them in the wrong place at different times of the day."

As for right price, the Price Company's stores are aided by their no-frills design and volume buying—with limited variety. At Nordstrom, customers pay for no-hassle shopping (smoothed by personal service) and wide variety. Select the ingredients to blend a right price recipe for your "store."

"The same six criteria apply to all three of the basic elements [the physical plant, the merchandise, and the employees], and we constantly evaluate] the mix," says Sol Price. "That's the name of the game."

Your Customer Relationships Reflect Your Employee Relationships

My "I'M FIRST" system says, "Your relationship with your customer reflects how you manage your company." That is evident at the Price Company. It is a democratic, open, honest, straightforward, plebeian, down-to-earth organization. That is how the customer is treated. And that is how the company is managed.

"Everybody uses first names," Price said. "There is no 'Mister Price.' I'm the only person in the company who wears a tie. They all come in, basically, in work clothes. Nobody has a special parking place. Nobody has a special garage. Nobody has a special toilet. Those things have as great an impact on employee enthusiasm and loyalty as anything."

Everyone in the company is an associate. No one is afraid of his or her boss, and no one is afraid to speak out. A customer-driven company requires the openness that allows for the free flow of feedback from employees to management and vice versa.

There are other examples of the atmosphere of equality within the organization. "When the chairman travels on company business, he never sends his expenses in to the company," Price said. "When the CEO travels, he charges the company for coach, but he pays first class himself. When we go away on a company retreat, we pay for dinner ourselves. Little things like that indicate to everybody that 'Management isn't setting themselves aside from the rest of us. They're not a group of aristocrats.'"

This attitude carries over to how the firm's customers are treated: "We have a philosophy that we never sell anything under cost. For example, around back-to-school time, all the other merchants will take the school notebook paper and sell it below cost. We carry it. But we put up a sign saying that we don't believe in selling things below cost. We tell you that many places sell it at below cost, and we advise you to buy the stuff there." Things like that, Price said, build credibility. The customers will say, "We trust these people." Another way that the Price Company translates its philosophy to its customers is reflected in what Sol Price calls its "liberal refund policy. Bring the stuff back, tell us what's wrong with it. We give you a credit slip, you take it to the cashier and get your money. You don't have to buy something else."

From this unpretentious style, Price said, comes "the purest kind of advertising, which is the unsolicited testimonial.

"It's important to know what you're doing and not be so

uncertain of your role as a merchant that every time somebody does something a little bit different, you feel you have to copy them and take them on," Price said. "Pretty soon, you, your employees, and your customers have a confused picture of what you are." If you know what your role is and stick with what you do well, he contends, your identity will become clear to your employees, customers, and distributors. They will know that they can count on you. That is what creates a loyal customer and loyal employees.

The "I'M FIRST" system helps you establish and maintain that core identity. Its emphasis on integration (chapter 2) influences every decision and constantly corrects your course toward your target customer. By showing you how to look at yourself from the customer's point of view, integration can turn each conscious (or subconscious) customer decision in your favor.

Your newfound sense of mission (chapter 3) guides you as you manage your company. The package of *values* that comes with your product is unsurpassed in your industry.

Gathering feedback (chapter 4) helps you to keep your customers coming back. You create your competitive edge by staying close to your customer and what she is thinking and feeling.

In discussing interviewing (chapter 5), we explored how to hire the kind of people who will succeed in your company in the long run. And I have shown you how to keep them focused on *your* goal of customer service by using rewards (chapter 6), support (chapter 7), and training (chapter 8).

The "I'M FIRST" system provides a clear plan for your workplace that will let you shatter the limitations on your career—and on your profits.

All of that . . . from putting your customer first.

APPENDIX I

"I'M FIRST" IN A NUTSHELL

A streamlined, cost-effective system for competing and winning in today's customer-driven market.

INTEGRATION	Is the customer service goal totally integrated throughout your organization? When customer service is the single element against which all decisions are measured, your company becomes like an immune system: "toxic to pests" that erode your customer base.
MISSION	Do you run the organization, or does it run you? Learn strategies for picking your priorities—and forging an organization that succeeds today, tomorrow, and far down the road.
FEEDBACK	Kill the complaint department! Develop innovative techniques for getting feedback from customers and employees—in a form you can put to *immediate use without major cost*.

INTERVIEWING	Hiring is expensive; firing is exorbitant. Hire the right people, keep the people you hire, and make your recruitment and hiring strategies work every time.
REWARD	You can institute a system of rewards and incentives that benefit the employees *and* the organization, creating an upward pressure for high performance.
SUPPORT	Do your employees have the leeway they need to defuse high-voltage customer situations? Do your regulations generate business, or impede it? You can develop regulations that actually *enforce* top-notch service.
TRAINING	Train your staff to create a priceless "golden handcuff" with the customer, garnering repeat business and market share as never before.

SAMPLE EMPLOYEE FEEDBACK SURVEY
SAMPLE CUSTOMER FEEDBACK SURVEY

The surveys that follow may help you in formulating your own customer and employee feedback surveys. The customer survey included here was designed by Sewell Village Cadillac in Dallas, Texas, and is used by permission. The employee survey was formulated by the *Los Angeles Times*, and also is used with permission.

The format of these surveys has been changed slightly for readability and printing requirements, but their content has not been materially altered.

Los Angeles Times
EMPLOYEE SURVEY

Times Employees:

Enclosed is a brief questionnaire which asks a set of questions about how satisfied you are with the company, your department, your supervisors, and your employee benefits.

A summary of the results will appear in "Among Ourselves" [an employee newsletter]. In addition, we will refer to the results whenever there are decisions to be made about the topics covered in the survey.

The survey is completely confidential. So please do not sign your name or otherwise identify yourself. You should return the survey within the next few days, using the postage-paid envelope provided.

Thank you in advance for your participation . . . your opinions about the company are valuable to me. I believe in the importance of striving constantly to achieve and to sustain an environment of excellence in all aspects of our employee relations programs.

October 1987

PLEASE NOTE—
To assure these questionnaires will be processed on a confidential basis, please **do not sign your name.** All questionnaires are to be mailed directly to MSI International. This reputable research firm will process the survey data. All responses will be tabulated by **groups of employees only—not by individuals.**

Please circle the number which corresponds to your answer in each question.

GENERAL OPINIONS

1. **Looking at The Times in general as compared with other employers, would you say it is:**

   1 About the best
   2 Much better than most
   3 About the same as most
   4 Not as good as most

2. **How satisfied are you with your job or the kind of work you do?**

   1 Very satisfied
   2 Somewhat satisfied
   3 Neither satisfied nor dissatisfied
   4 Somewhat dissatisfied
   5 Very dissatisfied

3. **I consider my future opportunities at The Times to be:**

   1 Excellent
   2 Good
   3 Fair
   4 Poor
   5 Not concerned about future advancement

Your comments would be appreciated:

_____
_____
_____

4. **How do you rate The Times in its effort to provide steady employment?**

   1 Excellent
   2 Good
   3 Fair
   4 Poor

5. How do you feel about your present rate of pay compared with rates paid for similar work by OTHER COMPANIES?

1 Higher
2 About the same
3 Lower

6. Which statement best describes how your supervisors act when there is a problem with employee behavior in your department?

1 Supervisors are too strict with all employees
2 There is inconsistency—some employees are treated fairly, others are not
3 No problem—employees are treated the same and the treatment is generally fair
4 Our supervisors are not strict enough—they do not seem to want to confront employees when there are problems

Your comments would be appreciated:

_____

_____

_____

7. How well do you feel you are informed about The Times and your department activities? *(Please circle ONE answer for EACH ITEM.)*

	The Times Activities	Department Activities
Well informed	1	1
Usually informed	2	2
Seldom informed	3	3
Poorly informed	4	4

8. As time goes by, do you find yourself more satisfied or less satisfied to be working at The Times?

1 More satisfied
2 No difference
3 Less satisfied

Why is that?

_____

_____

_____

YOUR COMPANY AND ITS POLICIES

We'd like your frank opinion of what The Times' strong and weak points are, as you see them. Please give careful thought to the following lists of personnel practices, benefits and working conditions.

BENEFITS

---

9. How do you rate The Times on the following benefits? *(Please circle ONE answer for EACH ITEM).*

	Excellent	Good	Fair	Poor	Not Eligible
INSURANCE PROGRAMS					
a) Group Life Insurance	1	2	3	4	5
b) Medical Insurance	1	2	3	4	5
c) Long Term Disability Insurance	1	2	3	4	5
d) Dental Insurance	1	2	3	4	5
e) Claims Processing	1	2	3	4	5
f) Vision Care	1	2	3	4	5
g) Prescription Card Service	1	2	3	4	5
h) Psychiatric Coverage	1	2	3	4	5
i) Alcohol/Drug Rehabilitation	1	2	3	4	5
RETIREMENT PROGRAM					
j) Pension Plan/ESOP	1	2	3	4	5
k) Past Service Improvement	1	2	3	4	5

l) Savings Plus Plan	1	2	3	4	5

TIME OFF WITH PAY

m) Number of paid holidays	1	2	3	4	5
n) Short term disability plan (sick days/insurance)	1	2	3	4	5
o) Vacation with pay	1	2	3	4	5
OVERALL BENEFITS	1	2	3	4	5

Your comments would be appreciated:

_____

_____

_____

WORKING CONDITIONS AND EMPLOYEE SERVICES

---

10. How do you rate the following employee services? *(Please circle ONE answer for EACH ITEM.)*

	Excellent	Good	Fair	Poor
a) Cafeteria	1	2	3	4
b) Credit Union	1	2	3	4
c) Employee parking	1	2	3	4
d) Medical Department	1	2	3	4
e) Employee Counseling Service	1	2	3	4
f) Service Award Program	1	2	3	4
g) Bus pass discounts	1	2	3	4
h) Employee Center	1	2	3	4

Your comments would be appreciated:

_____
_____
_____

11. How do you rate the company's efforts in the following areas? *(Please circle ONE answer for EACH ITEM.)*

	Excellent	Good	Fair	Poor
a) Accident prevention and safety	1	2	3	4
b) Method of handling employee grievances	1	2	3	4
c) Recognition of you as an individual	1	2	3	4
d) Administration of the Suggestion Plan	1	2	3	4
e) Equal employment	1	2	3	4
f) Tuition Refund Program	1	2	3	4
g) Security Services	1	2	3	4

Your comments would be appreciated:

_____
_____
_____

12. Do you think you would be better off if The Times were a union shop rather than an open shop?

1 Yes
2 No
3 Wouldn't make any difference
4 Don't know

Your comments would be appreciated:

_____
_____
_____

13. The following have been added or changed in the past two years. What are your opinions of each? *(Please circle ONE answer for EACH ITEM.)*

	Excellent	Good	Fair	Poor	Not Aware Of	Not Interested
a) Drug & alcohol policy	1	2	3	4	5	6
b) Smoking policy	1	2	3	4	5	6
c) TEAMS program	1	2	3	4	5	6
d) Pre-retirement counseling	1	2	3	4	5	6
e) Wellness program	1	2	3	4	5	6
f) Employee picnics/open houses	1	2	3	4	5	6
g) Personal enrichment programs (Aerobics, photography, Investment in Excellence, etc.)	1	2	3	4	5	6
h) Increased overtime pay for work on Christmas, New Year's Day & Thanksgiving	1	2	3	4	5	6
i) Medical insurance available to early retirees at age 60 (formerly age 62)	1	2	3	4	5	6
j) New Employee Benefits Statement	1	2	3	4	5	6
k) Recreational Activities	1	2	3	4	5	6

Your comments would be appreciated:

_____

_____

_____

_____

14. What other programs do you think we should add or improve?

_____

_____

_____

_____

15. What do you think of your immediate supervisor on the following points? *(Please circle ONE answer for EACH ITEM.)*

	Excellent	Good	Fair	Poor
a) Being helpful when you have a question or suggestion regarding your work	1	2	3	4
b) Showing you how to do your work better	1	2	3	4
c) Giving recognition when you do a good job	1	2	3	4
d) Being fair to everybody	1	2	3	4
e) Communicating objectives	1	2	3	4
f) Keeping promises	1	2	3	4
g) Explaining company policies	1	2	3	4
h) Listening to employees' opinions	1	2	3	4
i) Evaluating employees' performance	1	2	3	4
j) Conducting performance appraisal	1	2	3	4
k) Developing/promoting teamwork	1	2	3	4
l) Resolving problems/grievances	1	2	3	4
m) OVERALL performance of your immediate supervisor	1	2	3	4
n) Your DEPARTMENT'S OVERALL supervisory group	1	2	3	4

Your comments would be appreciated:

_____

_____

_____

_____

GENERAL QUESTIONS

16. What is the reputation of The Times among most of your immediate family and close friends?

	As a Newspaper	As an Employer
Excellent	1	1
Good	2	2
Fair	3	3
Poor	4	4

17. Please provide the following information about yourself. *(Please circle the appropriate number.)*

A. Present job status:

    1 Full-Time
    2 Part-Time
    3 Temporary

B. Which category best describes the type of work you do?

    1 Professional/technical
    2 Supervisory/managerial
    3 Sales
    4 Skilled craft or trade
    5 Semi-skilled or manual work
    6 Secretarial, clerical or other office work
    7 Other

C. Please indicate where you work:

    1 Los Angeles Facility
    2 Orange County Facility
    3 San Fernando Valley Facility
    4 San Diego
    5 Other location

D. Of which medical plan are you a member?

    1 Times Medical Plan (Aetna)
    2 Maxicare
    3 CIGNA
    4 Blue Cross Prudent Buyer
    5 None

E. Of which dental plan are you a member?

    1 Times Dental Plan (Aetna)
    2 Safeguard Dental Plan
    3 None

18. Please indicate your department.

_____

_____

_____

19. The following information about yourself is *optional*, but it will be very helpful in evaluating and comparing *group* opinions of all members of the Los Angeles Times Staff. *(Please circle ONE answer for EACH ITEM.)*

A. Age:

    1 Under 25
    2 25–44
    3 45 or over

B. Sex:

    1 Male
    2 Female

C. Length of Service:

    1 Under 1 year
    2 1 through 9 years
    3 10 years or more

D. Race/National Origin

    1 White
    2 Latino, Hispanic
    3 Black
    4 Asian, Pacific Islander
    5 American Indian

    6 Other _____

                                (please specify)

Additional comments and answers to questions in each of the following areas will be helpful.

Please describe any suggestions you believe would correct problem areas within your own department.

_____
_____
_____
_____

Please describe the things you like BEST about working for The Times.

_____
_____
_____
_____

What are some of the things you like LEAST about working for The Times?

_____
_____
_____
_____

Please describe anything that would make your job more fulfilling and meaningful:

_____
_____
_____
_____

Please outline any cost reduction steps that would make our company more successful:

_____

_____

_____

_____

Please describe any action ideas that you have to make the Los Angeles Times more efficient or more successful:

_____

_____

_____

_____

Additional comments about anything of particular interest to you:

_____

_____

_____

_____

THANK YOU. PLEASE DO NOT SIGN YOUR NAME.

The results of this survey as well as a cross section of all comments (positive, negative or neutral) will be shared with the entire employee population.

SEWELL VILLAGE CADILLAC

CUSTOMER QUESTIONNAIRE

1. Approximately how many times have you used our Service Department within the past year?

_____ times

WHEN YOU LAST USED OUR SERVICE DEPARTMENT

2. Did you have difficulty in finding the Service Department?

Yes _____ No _____

3. When you arrived at the service area, were you greeted promptly?

Yes _____ No _____

4. How were you treated when you entered our service reception area?

Very professional _____ Somewhat professional _____
Not at all professional _____

5. After you were greeted, approximately how long did you have to wait until your Service Advisor was available?

_____ minutes

6. Did you feel that the period of time you waited for your Service Advisor was excessive?

Yes _____ No _____

7. Did your Service Advisor explain things to you clearly?

Yes _____ No _____

8. Were you given a cost estimate of the charges for your automobile?

Yes _____ No _____

9. Were you given a time estimate as to when your automobile would be ready?

Yes _____ No _____

10. Sewell Village has various methods of payment available. Was this discussed with you?

Yes _____ No _____

11. Overall, how would you rate your satisfaction with your Service Advisor?
Very satisfied _____ Somewhat satisfied _____
Neither satisfied nor dissatisfied _____
Somewhat dissatisfied _____ Very dissatisfied _____

12. Are you aware that if you purchased your automobile *new* from Sewell Village, you can reserve a loan car?
Yes _____ No _____
(IF NO, SKIP TO Q. 15)

13. Are you familiar with the procedure of reserving a loan car?
Yes _____ No _____
(IF NO, SKIP TO Q. 15)

14. Did you call to reserve a loan car?
Yes _____ No _____
(IF NO, SKIP TO Q. 15)

14a. Did you feel that the loan car personnel were friendly?
Yes _____ No _____

14b. Was a loan car available when you needed it?
Yes _____ No _____

14c. Was there adequate gasoline in the loan car when you received it?
Yes _____ No _____

15. When you last used our Service Department, did you use our Courtesy Car?
Yes _____ No _____
(IF NO, SKIP TO Q. 19)

16. How satisfied were you with the cleanliness of the Courtesy Car?
Very satisfied _____ Somewhat satisfied _____
Neither satisfied nor dissatisfied _____
Somewhat dissatisfied _____ Very dissatisfied _____

17. Approximately how long did you wait for the Courtesy Car?
_____ minutes

18. Was the driver of the Courtesy Car professional?
Yes _____ No _____

19. When you last visited our Service Department, did you use our waiting area?

Yes _____ No _____
(IF NO, SKIP TO Q. 22)

20. Was our waiting area clean?

Yes _____ No _____

21. Was adequate seating available?

Yes _____ No _____

22. Did we call to inform you that your automobile was ready?

Yes _____ No _____
(IF YES, SKIP TO Q. 25)

23. How many rings did it take us to answer the telephone?

#_____ rings

24. Did we return your calls promptly?

Yes _____ No _____

25. Were we polite over the telephone?

Yes _____ No _____

26. Were we helpful over the telephone?

Yes _____ No _____

27. Was the repair/service completed correctly the first time your automobile was brought in?

Yes _____ No _____

28. How would you describe your satisfaction with the repair/service at Sewell Village?

Very satisfied _____ Somewhat satisfied _____
Neither satisfied nor dissatisfied _____
Somewhat dissatisfied _____ Very dissatisfied _____

29. Was your Cadillac ready when promised?

Yes _____ No _____

30. Approximately how long did you have to wait in line at the Cashier window?

_____ minutes

31. Was the Cashier polite?

Yes _____ No _____

32. Was the Cashier helpful?

Yes _____ No _____

33. If you had questions about what was done to your automobile, were we able to answer those questions?

Yes _____ No _____

34. Were the actual repair/service charges less than or the same as the *final* estimate?

Yes _____ No _____

35. To your knowledge, were all applicable warranties considered and applied to the repairs?

Yes _____ No _____

36. After you left the Cashier window, approximately how long did you have to wait for your automobile?

_____ minutes

37. Did the cashier clearly explain where your automobile would be delivered?

Yes _____ No _____

38. Was there a person waiting for you at your automobile when it was brought up to you?

Yes _____ No _____

(IF NO, SKIP TO Q.42)

39. Was that person friendly?

Yes _____ No _____

40. How would you rate that person's appearance?

Excellent _____ Good _____

Average _____ Poor _____

41. Did that person say "thank you"?

Yes _____ No _____

42. Did we get your automobile dirty during its servicing?

Yes _____ No _____

43. Our quality control department inspects every automobile we work on. Did you find an inspector's "thank you" card in your automobile?

Yes _____ No _____

44. Overall, how satisfied are you with Sewell Village's Service Department?

Very satisfied _____ Somewhat satisfied _____

Neither satisfied nor dissatisfied _____

Somewhat dissatisfied _____ Very dissatisfied _____

45. Did you buy your automobile from Sewell Village?

Yes _____ No _____

45a. If "yes", did you purchase your car new or used?

New _____ Used _____

45b. If purchased elsewhere, which dealer?

_____

46. What is the model year of your automobile?

19_____

47. Would you recommend the Sewell Village Service Department to a friend?

Yes _____ No _____

48. What is your Service Advisor's name?

_____

49. Did any one staff member, through outstanding service, make your visit more enjoyable?_____

_____

_____

50. Would you be interested in participating in our advisory panel?

Yes _____ No _____

Do you have any suggestions as to how Sewell Village could better serve you?

_____

_____

_____

_____

Thank you for taking the time to tell us about your service experience at Sewell Village. Our Quality Statement is: We will deliver 100 percent defect-free goods and services on time.

SAMPLE EMPLOYEE CONTRACT AND PRE-EMPLOYMENT INQUIRY GUIDELINES

The employee contract that follows was developed by Home Federal and is used by permission. The pre-employment Inquiry Guidelines shown here are provided by the State of California. Each of these may prove helpful to you as you design your own policies regarding employee recruitment and relations.

The format of these items has been changed slightly for readability and printing requirements, but their content has not been materially altered.

HOME FEDERAL EMPLOYEE CONTRACT

It's up to you . . .

What you make of your new job . . .
how much you enjoy doing it . . . how successful you are.
These things are all up to you.

As a corporation, Home Federal has a job to do. *Our* job is to provide the best possible financial services to our customers. Doing that job well is what keeps us in business . . . and enables us to offer you an excellent career opportunity as part of our sales team.

Your job, as part of Home Federal's marketing and sales team, is to act on our behalf, as our official representative: to ensure that customers receive the kind of courteous service they expect and deserve.

You may be the *only* contact a customer has with Home Federal. That customer's decision to continue banking with us could depend entirely on *you* . . . the courtesies you extend . . . the enthusiasm you express . . . all the little things that make the difference between an average job and an exceptional sales effort.

Home Federal's decision to hire you, and your decision to accept a position, requires that certain goals be established. These include, but are not limited to:

Home Federal's goals, as employer:

1. To encourage your professional development through training and career opportunities
2. To keep you up-to-date and informed on all aspects of new and existing Home Federal products
3. To give you feedback that will enable you to improve your performance and success
4. To continue to investigate new technologies, systems, and service innovations that can assist you in performing your job
5. To provide you with effective marketing materials to facilitate your sales efforts
6. To motivate customer response and interest through effective marketing efforts, thus providing you with ample opportunity to perform your sales function

Human Resources Director	Marketing Director

Employee goals, as an official representative:

1. To demonstrate at all times a professional manner and appearance.
2. To greet customers to my area, making them feel welcome and comfortable.
3. To be prompt, courteous, and friendly in serving customers. To use the customer's name whenever possible.
4. To adopt a problem-solving attitude in handling customer transactions and inquiries. To take time to assess each customer's needs, and when appropriate, to recommend specific Home Federal accounts and services.
5. To keep up-to-date on Home Federal products and provide customers with accurate information on all Home Federal accounts. To make a serious effort to find the right answers to all customer questions.
6. To be familiar with all organizational procedures, so that account servicing and transactions are handled with minimum error and delay.
7. To follow up on all inquiries and customer communications to the extent necessary to ensure customer satisfaction.
8. To be familiar with all ongoing advertising and promotional campaigns and to support these efforts.
9. To keep and accurately report necessary customer demographic information, in support of corporate marketing efforts.
10. To attempt to convert all customers to multi-service users.

I acknowledge receipt of this document.

Employee Signature	Date

Remember . . . your success is Home Federal's success. And vice versa. Let's work hard together to make it happen.

Welcome to Home Federal Country!

STATE OF CALIFORNIA

PRE-EMPLOYMENT INQUIRY GUIDELINES

The California Fair Employment and Housing Act prohibits any non-job-related inquiry, either verbal or through the use of an application form, which directly or indirectly limits a person's employment opportunities because of race, color, religion, national origin, ancestry, medical condition (cancer-related), physical handicap, marital status, sex, or age (40 +). The regulations of the Fair Employment and Housing Commission define this to include any question which:

- Identifies a person on a basis covered by the Act

or

- Results in the disproportionate screening out of members of a protected group

or

- Is not a valid predictor of successful job performance.

It is the employer's right to establish job-related requirements and to seek the most qualified individual for the job. It is presumed that the information obtained through application forms and interviews is used by the employer in making selection and assignment decisions. For this reason, the employer should make only those inquiries necessary to determine the applicant's eligibility to be considered for employment. Documents required for legitimate business purposes which reveal protected information (such as birth certificates, naturalization papers, or medical histories) may be requested at the point of hire, not before. (The point of hire is reached once the employer has decided to hire and so informs the applicant.)

This guide is not intended to be an exhaustive compilation of all acceptable and unacceptable inquiries. The examples listed are representative of questions frequently asked. Those considered unacceptable are likely to limit the employment opportunities of persons protected by the Fair Employment and Housing Act. Answers to questions on pre-employment inquiries can be obtained by calling your nearest Fair Employment and Housing office.

PRE-EMPLOYMENT INQUIRY GUIDELINES

ACCEPTABLE	SUBJECT	UNACCEPTABLE
Name	**NAME**	Maiden name.
"Have you ever used another name? /or/ "Is any additional information relative to change of name, use of an assumed name, or nickname necessary to enable a check on your work and education record? If yes, please explain."		
Place of residence.	**RESIDENCE**	"Do you own or rent your home?"
Statement that hire is subject to verification that applicant meets legal age requirements.	**AGE**	Age.
		Birthdate.
"If hired can you show proof of age?"		Dates of attendance or completion of elementary or high school.
"Are you over eighteen years of age?"		Questions which tend to identify applicants over age 40.
"If under eighteen, can you, after employment, submit a work permit?"		
"Can you, after employment, submit verification of your legal right to work in the United States?" /or/ Statement that such proof may be required after employment.	**BIRTHPLACE, CITIZENSHIP**	Birthplace of applicant, applicant's parents, spouse, or other relatives.
		"Are you a U.S. citizen?" /or/ Citizenship of applicant, applicant's parents, spouse, or other relatives.
		Requirements that applicant produce naturalization, first papers, or alien card *prior to employment.*

222

Languages applicant reads, speaks, or writes, if use of a language other than English is relevant to the job for which applicant is applying.	**NATIONAL ORIGIN**	Questions as to nationality, lineage, ancestry, national origin, descent, or parentage of applicant, applicant's parents, or spouse.
		"What is your mother tongue?" /or/ Language commonly used by applicant.
		How applicant acquired ability to read, write, or speak a foreign language.
Name and address of parent or guardian if applicant is a minor.	**SEX, MARITAL STATUS, FAMILY**	Questions which indicate applicant's sex.
		Questions which indicate applicant's marital status.
Statement of company policy regarding work assignment of employees who are related		Number and/or ages of children or dependents.
		Provisions for child care.
		Questions regarding pregnancy, child bearing, or birth control.
		Name or address of relative, spouse, or children of adult applicant.
		"With whom do you reside?" /or/ "Do you live with your parents?"
	RACE, COLOR	Questions as to applicant's race or color.
		Questions regarding applicant's complexion or color of skin, eyes, hair

223

ACCEPTABLE	SUBJECT	UNACCEPTABLE
Statement that photograph may be required after employment.	PHYSICAL DESCRIPTION, PHOTO-GRAPH	Questions as to applicant's height and weight. Require applicant to affix a photograph to application. Request applicant, at his or her option, to submit a photograph. Require a photograph after interview but before employment.
Statement by employer that offer may be made contingent on applicant passing a job-related physical examination. "Do you have any physical condition or handicap which may limit your ability to perform the job applied for? If yes, what can be done to accommodate your limitation?"	PHYSICAL CONDITION, HANDICAP	Questions regarding applicant's general medical condition, state of health, or illnesses. Questions regarding receipt of Workers' Compensation. "Do you have any physical disabilities or handicaps?"
Statement by employer of regular days, hours, or shifts to be worked.	RELIGION	Questions regarding applicant's religion. Religious days observed /or/ "Does your religion prevent you from working weekends or holidays?"
"Have you ever been convicted of a felony?" Such a question must be accompanied by a statement that a conviction will not necessarily disqualify an applicant from employment.	ARREST, CRIMINAL RECORD	Arrest record /or/ "Have you ever been arrested?"

224

	BONDING	Statement that bonding is a condition of hire.	Questions regarding refusal or cancellation of bonding.
	MILITARY SERVICE	Questions regarding relevant skills acquired during applicant's U.S. military service.	General questions regarding military services such as dates, and type of discharge.
			Questions regarding service in a foreign military.
	ECONOMIC STATUS		Questions regarding applicant's current or past assets, liabilities, or credit rating, including bankruptcy or garnishment.
	ORGANIZATIONS, ACTIVITIES	"Please list job-related organizations, clubs, professional societies, or other associations to which you belong—you may omit those which indicate your race, religious creed, color, national origin, ancestry, sex, or age."	"List all organizations, clubs, societies, and lodges to which you belong."
	REFERENCES	"By whom were you referred for a position here?" Names of persons willing to provide professional and/or character references for applicant.	Questions of applicant's former employers or acquaintances which elicit information specifying the applicant's race, color, religious creed, national origin, ancestry, physical handicap, medical condition, marital status, age, or sex.
	NOTICE IN CASE OF EMERGENCY	Name and address of person to be notified in case of accident or emergency.	Name and address of relative to be notified in case of accident or emergency.

ABOUT THE AUTHOR

Linda Silverman Goldzimer is president of Linda Goldzimer Consulting Group, which provides feature presentations, staff development training, and consultation for organizations throughout the world.

Ms. Goldzimer is a dynamic speaker of international caliber who has also published many articles in magazines, newspapers, and trade journals. Her consulting group's areas of expertise are: customer relationships, leadership development, team building, and communication skills.

The Linda Goldzimer Consulting Group has offices in San Diego, California, and in the New York City area.

San Diego address:

Linda Goldzimer Consulting Group
P.O. Box 821
Del Mar, CA 92014
(619) 481-7223
FAX #619-481-6152

New York address:

Linda Goldzimer Consulting Group
32 Treeview Drive
Melville, NY 11747
(516) 367-4998
FAX #516-367-6631

INDEX